W9-CVY-256

Woman's Realm Book of

CAKES &
DESSERTS

Woman's Realm Book of
CAKES & DESSERTS

HAMLYN

London · New York · Sydney · Toronto

Photography on pages 2, 6, 10, 14, 23, 55, 63, 87, 134, 143 and 151
by Paul Williams

Published by
The Hamlyn Publishing Group Limited
London · New York · Sydney · Toronto
Astronaut House, Feltham, Middlesex, England
© Copyright IPC Magazines Limited 1981

Reprinted 1982

ISBN 0 600 32230 0

All rights reserved. No part of this publication may be reproduced,
stored in a retrieval system, or transmitted, in any form or by any
means, electronic, mechanical, photocopying, recording or otherwise,
without the permission of the copyright holder and The Hamlyn Publishing
Group Limited.

Phototypeset by Servis Filmsetting Ltd, Manchester
Printed in Czechoslovakia
52 053/2

CONTENTS

INTRODUCTION

From the Woman's Realm kitchen comes a very special collection of cakes and desserts – all tried, tested and thoroughly enjoyed. And we're delighted to be sharing them with you.

We've made sure that there's something here to suit every occasion, from a homely rubbed-in cake for a family tea to a splendid soufflé that will delight and impress at a dinner party.

You'll find a wide and interesting range of recipes including superb traditional British cakes, good old-fashioned puddings, delectable ice creams, exciting recipes from abroad and gourmet desserts.

Many of the recipes are quick and easy, tailored to the needs of working wives and busy mums but there are more complicated ones too for when you are in a creative mood and have time to spare. In every case, the recipes are clearly explained so even a beginner can enjoy the real satisfactions of producing a spectacular dish.

We're starting off our recipe collection with:

A bun feast: Here you'll find cheerful little cakes the kids will love and that are just the right size to pop in the lunchbox. There are some special treats too, like doughnuts, brandy snaps and meringues with really tempting fillings.

Family favourites: These include some of our best-of-British specialities like lardy cake and Simnel cake, as well as plenty of budget-minded cakes to enjoy every day.

Special occasion gâteaux: Help yourself to a slice of the luxury life! We haven't skimped on gorgeous real cream, nuts, chocolate and brandy. Add to that lots of clever ideas for filling and decorating and you end up with cakes you'll be really proud to serve.

The pleasures of pastry: A section devoted to making and using all kinds of pastry. You'll find heartwarming fruit pies, pretty tartlets and flans.

Cold and delicious: The double delight of ice cream – simple to make and very delicious to eat. Plus lovely fruit desserts and irresistible jellies, blancmanges and mousses.

Winter warmers: A tempting choice of substantial puddings to satisfy a family – steamy sponges, baked treats and traditional favourites to round off any meal. Most cake mixtures will fit an 18–20 cm/7–8 inch cake tin, or set of sandwich tins. You will need a baking sheet and small patty tins, or paper cake cases. The most useful size of flan ring or dish is 20 cm/8 inches. If you are buying a basin for steamed puddings, go for the 1.25-litre/2-pint size. Pie dishes and pie plates will be needed too.

To add those important finishing touches, it's a good idea to have chocolate vermicelli, blanched almonds, walnut halves, angelica and glacé cherries. A supply of ice cream in the freezer and some dried and canned fruit and you'll always be able to concoct an interesting dessert.

Throughout the book you'll find great ideas for accompaniments and for decorating your cakes and desserts. Add to that foolproof methods and easy-to-follow instructions and you'll always be able to cook up a treat.

USEFUL FACTS AND FIGURES

Notes on metrication

In this book quantities are given in metric and Imperial measures. Exact conversion from Imperial to metric measures does not usually give very convenient working quantities and so the metric measures have been rounded off into units of 25 grams. The table below shows the recommended equivalents.

Ounces	Approx g to nearest whole figure	Recommended conversion to nearest unit of 25
1	28	25
2	57	50
3	85	75
4	113	100
5	142	150
6	170	175
7	198	200
8	227	225
9	255	250
10	283	275
11	312	300
12	340	350
13	368	375
14	396	400
15	425	425
16 (1 lb)	454	450
17	482	475
18	510	500
19	539	550
20 ($1\frac{1}{4}$ lb)	567	575

Note: When converting quantities over 20 oz first add the appropriate figures in the centre column, then adjust to the nearest unit of 25. As a general guide, 1 kg (1000 g) equals 2.2 lb or about 2 lb 3 oz. This method of conversion gives good results in nearly all cases, although in certain pastry and cake recipes a more accurate conversion is necessary to produce a balanced recipe.

Liquid measures The millilitre has been used in this book and the following table gives a few examples.

Imperial	Approx ml to nearest whole figure	Recommended ml
$\frac{1}{4}$ pint	142	150ml
$\frac{1}{2}$ pint	283	300ml
$\frac{3}{4}$ pint	425	450ml
1 pint	567	600ml
$1\frac{1}{2}$ pints	851	900ml
$1\frac{3}{4}$ pints	992	1000ml (1 litre)

Spoon measures All spoon measures given in this book are level unless otherwise stated.

Can sizes At present, cans are marked with the exact (usually to the nearest whole number) metric equivalent of the Imperial weight of the contents, so we have followed this practice when giving can sizes.

Oven temperatures

The table below gives recommended equivalents.

	°C	°F	Gas Mark
Very cool	110	225	$\frac{1}{4}$
	120	250	$\frac{1}{2}$
Cool	140	275	1
	150	300	2
Moderate	160	325	3
	180	350	4
Moderately hot	190	375	5
	200	400	6
Hot	220	425	7
	230	450	8
Very hot	240	475	9

Notes for American and Australian users

In America the 8-oz measuring cup is used. In Australia metric measures are now used in conjunction with the standard 250-ml measuring cup. The Imperial pint, used in Britain and Australia, is 20 fl oz, while the American pint is 16 fl oz. It is important to remember that the Australian tablespoon differs from both the British and American tablespoons; the table below gives a comparison. The British standard tablespoon, which has been used throughout this book, holds 17.7 ml, the American 14.2 ml, and the Australian 20 ml. A teaspoon holds approximately 5 ml in all three countries.

British	American	Australian
1 teaspoon	1 teaspoon	1 teaspoon
1 tablespoon	1 tablespoon	1 tablespoon
2 tablespoons	3 tablespoons	2 tablespoons
$3\frac{1}{2}$ tablespoons	4 tablespoons	3 tablespoons
4 tablespoons	5 tablespoons	$3\frac{1}{2}$ tablespoons

An Imperial/American guide to solid and liquid measures

Solid measures

Imperial	American
1 lb butter or margarine	2 cups
1 lb flour	4 cups
1 lb granulated or castor sugar	2 cups
1 lb icing sugar	3 cups
8 oz rice	1 cup

Liquid measures

Imperial	American
$\frac{1}{4}$ pint liquid	$\frac{2}{3}$ cup liquid
$\frac{1}{2}$ pint	$1\frac{1}{4}$ cups
$\frac{3}{4}$ pint	2 cups
1 pint	$2\frac{1}{2}$ cups
$1\frac{1}{2}$ pints	$3\frac{3}{4}$ cups
2 pints	5 cups ($2\frac{1}{2}$ pints)

NOTE: WHEN MAKING ANY OF THE RECIPES IN THIS BOOK, ONLY FOLLOW ONE SET OF MEASURES AS THEY ARE NOT INTERCHANGEABLE.
It is generally recommended that, prior to cooking the recipes in this book, a brief pre-heating of the oven, up to ten minutes, is observed.

SMALL CAKES

Caramel Tops

Approximate preparation time: 20
minutes
Cooking time: 30 minutes
Makes 8

100 g/4 oz self-raising flour
75 g/3 oz margarine
50 g/2 oz castor sugar
1 large egg, beaten
2 tablespoons milk
100 g/4 oz icing sugar
few drops almond essence
100 g/4 oz granulated sugar

Place eight paper cases on a baking tray.

Sift the flour into a bowl, rub in half the margarine and stir in the sugar. Add the egg and 1 tablespoon of milk. Mix well. Spoon into the cases and bake in a moderately hot oven (190°C, 375°F, Gas Mark 5) for about 25 minutes. Leave to cool.

Sift the icing sugar and beat in the rest of the milk and margarine. Add a few drops of almond essence. Put the granulated sugar in a pan with 3 tablespoons water and stir over a low heat until dissolved. Boil steadily until golden. Pour the mixture on to a lightly oiled baking tray. Leave until cold and hard. Break up into pieces with a rolling pin. Fit a piping bag with a medium star nozzle. Fill the bag with the icing and pipe a swirl on each bun. Top with pieces of caramel.

These freeze well without the decoration. Store for up to 2 months and thaw for 4–5 hours.

Pineapple Buns

Approximate preparation time: 12
minutes
Cooking time: 20 minutes
Makes 12

50 g/2 oz margarine
50 g/2 oz castor sugar
1 large egg
$1\frac{1}{2}$ tablespoons pineapple jam
100 g/4 oz self-raising flour
75 g/3 oz icing sugar
12 sugar flowers (optional)

Put 12 paper cases in 12 patty tins, or on an ungreased baking tray.

Cream the margarine with the sugar until light and fluffy, then beat in the egg. Mix in the jam and fold in the flour. Spoon the mixture into the cases and bake in a moderately hot oven (190°C, 375°F, Gas Mark 5) for 20 minutes, or until golden. Sift the icing sugar and mix with about 1 tablespoon water to make a coating icing. When the buns are cool, spoon the icing on to the tops. If used, place the flowers in the centre of the icing. Eat within 3 days.

These buns freeze well. Store frozen for up to 2 months and thaw for 4–5 hours.

Raspberry Tops

Approximate preparation time: 20
minutes
Cooking time: 15–20 minutes
Makes 12

150 g/5 oz margarine
50 g/2 oz castor sugar
1 large egg
1 tablespoon raspberry jam
100 g/4 oz self-raising flour
$\frac{1}{4}$ teaspoon baking powder
100 g/4 oz icing sugar plus extra to
dust
1 tablespoon milk
few drops pink colouring

Place 12 paper cases in patty tins.

Cream 75 g/3 oz of the margarine with the sugar until light and fluffy. Beat the egg and add gradually to the creamed mixture, beating well. Beat in the jam. Sift the flour and baking powder over the top and fold in with a metal spoon. Divide the mixture between the cases and cook in a moderate oven (180°C, 350°F, Gas Mark 4) for 15–20 minutes, or until risen and golden.

When the buns are cool, slice the tops off carefully. Sift a little icing sugar over the tops.

Sift the icing sugar into a bowl and cream with the remaining margarine, the milk and colouring. When smooth, spoon or pipe the buttercream on to the cakes and put the lids back.

These cakes freeze well. Pack in a box or freezer container. Store for up to 2 months. Thaw for 4–5 hours.

A party idea

Instead of one large cake at a children's party, give each child a small cake complete with a candle.

Raspberry Tops

Orange Tops

Approximate preparation time: 20
minutes
Cooking time: 15–20 minutes
Makes 12

150 g/5 oz margarine
50 g/2 oz castor sugar
1 large egg
1 tablespoon jelly marmalade
100 g/4 oz self-raising flour
$\frac{1}{4}$ teaspoon baking powder
1 tablespoon milk
100 g/4 oz icing sugar plus extra to
dust
undiluted orange squash to taste
1 teaspoon grated orange rind

Follow the method for Raspberry tops, but omit the raspberry jam and use jelly marmalade instead. Add the orange squash to flavour the icing with the grated orange rind.

These freeze well; store for up to 2 months. Thaw for 4–5 hours

Rum Tops

Approximate preparation time: 20
minutes
Cooking time: 15–20 minutes
Makes 12

150 g/5 oz margarine
50 g/2 oz castor sugar
1 large egg
1 tablespoon raspberry jam
100 g/4 oz self-raising flour
$\frac{1}{4}$ teaspoon baking powder
1 tablespoon milk
100 g/4 oz icing sugar plus extra for
dusting
few drops rum essence

Make exactly as for Raspberry tops, but omit the colouring. Add rum essence to taste, or if you have some ordinary rum, use 2 teaspoons of this.

These freeze well. Store for up to 2 months. Thaw for 4–5 hours.

Lemon Curd Buns

Approximate preparation time: 20
minutes
Cooking time: 20–25 minutes
Makes 12

100 g/4 oz self-raising flour
pinch of salt
100 g/4 oz margarine
100 g/4 oz castor sugar
2 eggs, beaten
3 tablespoons plus 1 teaspoon
lemon curd
100 g/4 oz icing sugar
50 g/2 oz butter or soft margarine

Put 12 paper cases in patty tins or on an ungreased baking tray.

Sift the flour with the salt. Cream the margarine with the sugar until light and fluffy, then gradually add the eggs, beating well. Stir in 2 teaspoons of the lemon curd, then fold in the flour. Spoon the mixture into the cases and bake in a moderately hot oven (190°C, 375°F, Gas Mark 5) for 20–25 minutes. Leave to cool.

Sift the icing sugar and cream it with the butter or soft margarine and 1 teaspoon of the lemon curd. Fit a piping bag with a medium star nozzle. Fill the bag with the icing and pipe a ring on top of each cake. Fill the centre of the rings with the remaining lemon curd.

These buns may be frozen for up to 2 months. Thaw for 4–5 hours.

Variation
Instead of the lemon curd you could use orange jelly marmalade for a different taste.

Frosted Cakes

Approximate preparation time: 30
minutes
Cooking time: 25–30 minutes
Makes 9

175 g/6 oz margarine
175 g/6 oz castor sugar
3 large eggs plus 2 large egg whites
150 g/5 oz self-raising flour
25 g/1 oz cornflour
$\frac{1}{4}$ teaspoon baking powder
1 tablespoon milk
225 g/8 oz icing sugar
pinch of cream of tartar
9 walnut halves

Grease nine 8-cm/$3\frac{1}{2}$-inch patty tins or 18 smaller tins.

Cream the margarine with the sugar until light and fluffy. Beat the whole eggs together and add gradually to the creamed mixture, beating all the time. Sift the flour, cornflour and baking powder over the mixture and fold in with a metal spoon. Mix in the milk. Spoon the mixture into the tins. Bake in a moderately hot oven (190°C, 375°F, Gas Mark 5) for 25–30 minutes for large tins, 15 minutes for smaller ones. Leave to cool.

Sift the icing sugar with the cream of tartar and whisk with the egg whites until very thick. This will take 5–10 minutes. Cover the cakes with the whisked mixture and put a walnut half on each. Eat within 1 day.

These cakes may be frozen without the frosting. Store frozen for up to 2 months and thaw for 4–5 hours. Add the frosting when thawed.

Lemon and Cherry Cup Cakes

Approximate preparation time: 25 minutes
Cooking time: 15 minutes
Makes 8

75 g/3 oz self-raising flour
50 g/2 oz margarine
50 g/2 oz castor sugar
1 egg
milk to mix
175 g/6 oz icing sugar
100 g/4 oz unsalted butter
3 tablespoons lemon curd
3 tablespoons cherry jam

Put eight paper cases in patty tins.

Sift the flour. Cream the margarine and sugar until light and fluffy. Beat the egg and gradually add to the creamed mixture. Fold in the flour with enough milk to make a fairly soft dropping consistency. Spoon the mixture into the cases. Bake in a moderate oven (180°C, 350°F, Gas Mark 4) for 15 minutes, or until firm.

Sift the icing sugar and beat with the butter until light and creamy. Fit a piping bag with a medium star nozzle. Fill the bag with the icing and pipe around the edge of each cake. Fill the centre of each top with jam.

You can freeze these cakes undecorated, for up to 2 months. Thaw for about 5 hours in their wrappings. Then add the butter icing and jam or curd as suggested in the recipe.

Honey and Almond Cakes

Approximate preparation time: 15 minutes
Cooking time: 20–25 minutes
Makes 14

75 g/3 oz plain flour
1 teaspoon baking powder
50 g/2 oz cornflour
pinch of salt
100 g/4 oz castor sugar
100 g/4 oz margarine
2 eggs
2 teaspoons clear honey
$\frac{1}{2}$ teaspoon almond essence
1 tablespoon milk
icing sugar to dust

Grease 14 plain or fluted patty tins and dust with a little flour and castor sugar.

Sift the flour with the baking powder, cornflour and salt. Cream the sugar and margarine until light and fluffy. Beat the eggs and gradually add to the creamed mixture, beating all the time. Stir in the honey and almond essence. Fold in the sifted flour and add the milk.

Spoon the mixture into the tins and bake in a moderately hot oven (190°C, 375°F, Gas Mark 5) for 20–25 minutes.

Turn out and cool on a wire rack and dust the tops with sifted icing sugar.

These cakes can be frozen and stored for up to 2 months. Thaw for 4–5 hours.

Honey Notes

Honey gives a delicious flavour to cakes. It was used as a sweetener in cooking before sugar was imported into Britain.

Cakes made with honey seem to keep longer, too – provided they are stored in an airtight box.

Ginger and Lemon Buns

Approximate preparation time: 15 minutes
Cooking time: 15–20 minutes
Makes 12

2 teaspoons golden syrup
50 g/2 oz castor sugar
50 g/2 oz butter
1 egg
75 g/3 oz self-raising flour
$\frac{1}{4}$ teaspoon ground ginger
100 g/4 oz icing sugar
2 teaspoons lemon juice
few drops yellow colouring (optional)
angelica (optional)

Put 12 paper cases on a baking tray.

Mix the golden syrup, sugar and butter together and cream until light and fluffy. Beat the egg and gradually add to the creamed mixture. Sift the flour with the ginger and fold into the mixture using a metal spoon. Spoon the mixture into the cases and bake in a moderately hot oven (190°C, 375°F, Gas Mark 5) for 15 minutes. Leave to cool.

Sift the icing sugar into a bowl and add the lemon juice and colouring if used. If necessary add a little water to make a smooth icing. Spoon the icing on to the buns and decorate with angelica if liked. These buns will keep for up to 2 days in an airtight tin.

These buns may be frozen before they are iced. Store for up to 2 months. Thaw for about 5 hours.

Coffee Swirls

Approximate preparation time: 20
minutes
Cooking time: 15–20 minutes
Makes 12

75 g/3 oz margarine
75 g/3 oz castor sugar
1 large egg
3 teaspoons instant coffee powder
$\frac{1}{2}$ teaspoon ground mixed spice
100 g/4 oz self-raising flour
100 g/4 oz icing sugar

Put 12 paper cases on a baking tray.

Cream the margarine and sugar together until light and fluffy. Gradually add the egg, beating well. Dissolve 2 teaspoons of the coffee in 2 teaspoons hot water and beat into the creamed mixture. Sift the spice and flour over the mixture and fold in with a metal spoon. Spoon the mixture into the cases and bake in a moderately hot oven (190°C, 375°F, Gas Mark 5) for 15–20 minutes. Cool.

Mix the remaining coffee with 2 teaspoons hot water. Sift the icing sugar and work in the coffee. Add more water if necessary. Fit a piping bag with a fine nozzle and pipe patterns on top of the cold cakes.

These may be frozen without the icing for up to 2 months. Thaw for 4–5 hours.

Walnut and Ginger Cakes

Approximate preparation time: 20 minutes
Cooking time: 50 minutes
Makes 6

225 g/8 oz plain flour
50 g/2 oz walnut halves
pinch of salt
2 teaspoons ground ginger
$\frac{1}{2}$ teaspoon ground mixed spice
40 g/1$\frac{1}{2}$ oz granulated sugar
40 g/1$\frac{1}{2}$ oz lard
50 g/2 oz golden syrup
50 g/2 oz black treacle
3 tablespoons milk
$\frac{1}{2}$ teaspoon bicarbonate of soda
1 small egg
100 g/4 oz icing sugar

Grease a 15 × 20-cm/6 × 8-inch cake tin and line with greaseproof paper.

Sift the flour. Reserve six walnut halves, chop the rest finely and add to the flour. Add the salt, ginger, spice and sugar. Melt the lard in a pan with the syrup, treacle and 2 tablespoons of the milk. Dissolve the bicarbonate of soda in the remaining milk, pour the treacle mixture into the flour and mix well. Beat the egg and mix into the flour with the bicarbonate of soda. Pour into the prepared tin and cook in a moderate oven (180°C, 350°F, Gas Mark 4) for about 50 minutes. Cool then cut into six pieces.

Sift the icing sugar and add enough water to make an even coating mixture. Spoon on to the cakes and add the nuts.

Glacé icing

When adding colouring to glacé icing, drop it from tip of a skewer a drop at a time, and thus avoid too hectic a colour!

Blackcurrant Squares

Approximate preparation time: 25 minutes
Cooking time: 1 hour 10 minutes
Makes 9

250 g/9 oz soft margarine
75 g/3 oz castor sugar
50 g/2 oz soft brown sugar
3 large eggs
4 tablespoons blackcurrant jam
190 g/6$\frac{1}{2}$ oz self-raising flour
$\frac{1}{2}$ teaspoon ground mixed spice
200 g/7 oz icing sugar
1 tablespoon milk
2 drops vanilla essence

Grease a 20-cm/8-inch square cake tin and line with greaseproof paper.

Beat two-thirds of the margarine with the castor and brown sugars. Beat the eggs and add gradually, beating all the time. Beat in half the jam. Sift the flour and spice over the mixture and fold in with a metal spoon. Turn the mixture into the prepared tin and cook in a moderate oven (180°C, 350°F, Gas Mark 4) for about 1 hour 10 minutes. Turn on to a wire rack to cool, then cut into nine squares.

Cream the remaining margarine, sift the icing sugar and beat together until smooth. Beat in the milk and vanilla. Fit a piping bag with a small star nozzle and fill the bag with the icing. Pipe a design around the top of each square and spread jam on the top of each cake. Eat the same day.

These cakes may be frozen for up to 2 months. Thaw for 4–5 hours.

Variation
Instead of imitation butter icing, use American-type cream cheese for piping.

Teatime Squares

Approximate preparation time: 40
minutes
Cooking time: 45 minutes
Makes 9

50 g/2 oz butter
75 g/3 oz castor sugar
1 large egg
$\frac{1}{2}$ teaspoon vanilla essence
150 g/5 oz self-raising flour
pinch of salt
1 tablespoon milk
2 tablespoons raspberry jam
100 g/4 oz icing sugar
1 tablespoon cocoa powder
50 g/2 oz desiccated coconut

Grease a 15-cm/6-inch square cake tin and line with greaseproof paper.

Cream the butter and sugar together until light and fluffy. Beat the egg and add to the mixture gradually, beating all the time. Mix in the vanilla. Sift the flour on to the mixture and fold in with the salt and milk, using a metal spoon. Turn into the prepared tin and bake in a moderate oven (160°C, 325°F, Gas Mark 3) for about 45 minutes. Turn on to a wire rack to cool. Slice the cake into two layers and sandwich them together with the jam. Cut into nine squares.

Sift the icing sugar and cocoa together and add just enough hot water to make a smooth icing. Dip the squares in this and then in the coconut. Leave to set. Eat within 2 days.

These cakes may be frozen for up to 6 weeks. Thaw for 4–5 hours.

Variations
Use any variety of jam or lemon curd or marmalade to make an interesting filling.

Apple and Ginger Squares

Approximate preparation time: 25
minutes
Cooking time: 1$\frac{1}{2}$ hours
Makes 6

450 g/1 lb cooking apples
175 g/6 oz margarine
175 g/6 oz soft brown sugar
3 large eggs
2 tablespoons golden syrup
225 g/8 oz self-raising flour
1$\frac{1}{2}$ teaspoons ground ginger
$\frac{3}{4}$ teaspoon ground cinnamon
150 ml/$\frac{1}{4}$ pint double cream
(optional)

Grease a 20-cm/8-inch cake tin and line with greaseproof paper.

Peel, core and chop the apples. Cream the margarine and sugar together until light and fluffy. Add the eggs, one at a time, beating well. Beat in the syrup.

Sift the flour with the ginger and $\frac{1}{2}$ teaspoon of the cinnamon. Fold into the creamed mixture with the apples.

Turn the mixture into the prepared tin and cook in a moderate oven (180°C, 350°F, Gas Mark 4) for 1$\frac{1}{2}$ hours. Cool on a wire rack. Cut into six pieces when cool.

If using cream, whip it with the remaining cinnamon until thick. Fit a piping bag with a small star nozzle and fill with the cream. Pipe a line of cream on each cake.

These cakes may be frozen and stored for up to 2 months. Thaw for 4–5 hours. Be careful, when packing, that you do not damage the decoration.

Devonshire Splits

Approximate preparation time: 20
minutes
Cooking time: 20 minutes
Makes 12

**450 g/1 lb plain flour
large pinch of salt
25 g/1 oz castor sugar
75 g/3 oz margarine
15 g/$\frac{1}{2}$ oz fresh yeast
7 tablespoons lukewarm milk
7 tablespoons lukewarm water
1 small egg
6 tablespoons raspberry jam
150 ml/$\frac{1}{4}$ pint double cream or
clotted cream
25 g/1 oz icing sugar**

Sift the flour and salt into a bowl. Add the
sugar and rub in the margarine.

Cream the yeast with a little of the milk
then add the rest of the milk and the water.
Make a well in the centre of the flour and
pour in the yeast liquid.

Beat the egg and add to the liquid. Mix in
the flour to make a smooth dough. Turn out
on to a lightly floured surface and knead
well for 10 minutes. Put the dough in a large
bowl and place the whole in a large, lightly
oiled polythene bag. Leave in a warm place
until the dough has doubled in size. This will
take about 45 minutes.

Knead the dough for 2 minutes then
shape into 12 rounds. Arrange them on a
baking tray, allowing plenty of space between them. Leave in a warm place for 15
minutes to rise, then cook in a hot oven
(220°C, 425°F, Gas Mark 7) for 20 minutes
or until golden. Leave to cool.

If using double cream, whip it until quite
stiff. Split the buns and fill with jam and
cream. Sift the icing sugar over the tops.

Eat the filled buns the same day.

The unfilled buns can be frozen and
stored for up to 2 months. Thaw for 4–5
hours then fill as above.

Apple Doughnuts

Approximate preparation time: 25
minutes
Cooking time: 23–25 minutes
Makes 12

**225 g/8 oz cooking apples
75 g/3 oz granulated sugar
225 g/8 oz self-raising flour
$\frac{1}{2}$ teaspoon ground cinnamon
pinch of salt
50 g/2 oz margarine
4 tablespoons milk
oil for deep-frying
castor sugar to sprinkle**

Peel, core and slice the apples. Place in a
saucepan with the sugar and 2 tablespoons
water. Cover and simmer for 15 minutes or
until the apple is pulpy.

Strain the apple well in a sieve, letting all
the excess liquid run out. Allow to cool
completely.

Sift the flour with the cinnamon and salt,
rub in the margarine then mix in the apple
and milk to make a soft dough. Roll out on a
floured surface to 5 mm/$\frac{1}{4}$ inch thick and cut
out 6.5-cm/2$\frac{1}{2}$-inch rounds with a plain
cutter. Cut out the middle of each round
with a 2.5-cm/1-inch cutter and use the
centres to make more rings. Heat the oil to
190°C/375°F and fry the doughnuts in two
batches until golden and cooked through.
This will take about 5 minutes. Drain on
absorbent kitchen paper and sprinkle with
castor sugar.

Eat the same day, either hot or cold.

Remember to use very clean oil for frying
the doughnuts, not that used for fish and
chips!

Devonshire Splits

Chocolate Castle Cakes

Approximate preparation time: 20 minutes
Cooking time: 15–20 minutes
Makes 7

75 g/3 oz self-raising flour
$\frac{1}{4}$ teaspoon baking powder
1 tablespoon cocoa powder
50 g/2 oz soft margarine
50 g/2 oz castor sugar
1 large egg
4 tablespoons apricot jam
65 g/$2\frac{1}{2}$ oz chocolate vermicelli
double cream
glacé cherries and angelica for decoration (optional)

Grease seven dariole moulds and place on a baking tray.

Sift the flour into a bowl with the baking powder and cocoa. Add the margarine, sugar and egg and mix with a wooden spoon until smooth. Half-fill the prepared moulds with the mixture then bake in a moderate oven (160°C, 325°F, Gas Mark 3) for 15–20 minutes. Cool on a wire rack.

Heat and sieve the jam. Hold each cake on a skewer and brush with jam. Roll each cake in chocolate vermicelli.

Whip the cream until thick. Fit a piping bag with a medium star nozzle. Fill the bag with the cream and pipe a little on to each cake. Top with cherries and angelica if liked.

Freeze these cakes for up to 2 months. Thaw for 4–5 hours.

Variation

For a special occasion, prick the cakes and sprinkle with a little sherry before decorating.

Chocolate Triangles

Approximate preparation time: 25 minutes
Cooking time: 25 minutes
Makes 7

100 g/4 oz self-raising flour
15 g/$\frac{1}{2}$ oz cocoa powder
pinch of salt
25 g/1 oz plain chocolate
100 g/4 oz margarine
100 g/4 oz castor sugar
2 large eggs
175 g/6 oz icing sugar
50 g/2 oz cream cheese
1 tablespoon undiluted orange squash
15 g/$\frac{1}{2}$ oz chocolate vermicelli
angelica for decoration

Lightly grease a 19-cm/$7\frac{1}{2}$-inch sandwich tin and line the base with greaseproof paper.

Sift the flour with the cocoa and salt. Melt the chocolate in a small bowl over a pan of simmering water. Cream the margarine and sugar together until light and fluffy. Beat the eggs and mix into the creamed mixture gradually. Whisk in the melted chocolate and fold in the flour mixture using a metal spoon.

Turn the mixture into the prepared tin, smooth the top and cook in a moderately hot oven (190°C, 375°F, Gas Mark 5) for 25 minutes.

Sift the icing sugar and mix with the cream cheese and orange squash. Spread two-thirds of this over the cake. Fit a piping bag with a small star nozzle and fill the bag with the icing. Pipe a ring around the edge of the cake. Sprinkle the top with chocolate vermicelli. Cut the cake in wedges and decorate with angelica. Eat the same day.

These cakes may be frozen for up to 2 months. Thaw for 4–5 hours then eat the same day.

Coconut Macaroons

Approximate preparation time: 15 minutes
Cooking time: 45 minutes
Makes 12

2 large egg whites
175 g/6 oz castor sugar
20 g/$\frac{3}{4}$ oz cornflour
75 g/3 oz desiccated coconut
$\frac{1}{2}$ teaspoon almond essence
$\frac{1}{2}$ teaspoon vanilla essence (or use all almond essence)

Line two baking trays with foil or bakewell paper.

Whisk the egg whites until stiff and standing in peaks. Add the sugar, a little at a time, whisking continuously. Stir in the cornflour, coconut and essences. Place dessertspoons of the mixture on the prepared baking trays, leaving plenty of space between them. Bake in a cool oven (150°C, 300°F, Gas Mark 2) for 45 minutes. Cool and peel off any pieces of foil.

Store in an airtight tin.

Variation

These biscuits make a good base for trifles. Crumble them roughly and put in the base of a bowl. Sprinkle on a little fruit juice and sherry or cold black coffee. Continue as for an ordinary trifle, adding fruit, custard and cream.

Coconut Meringues

Approximate preparation time: 15 minutes
Cooking time: 3$\frac{1}{2}$ hours
Makes 9

2 large egg whites
100 g/4 oz castor sugar
25 g/1 oz desiccated coconut

Line a baking tray with foil. Whisk the egg whites until very stiff and standing in peaks. Add the sugar, a teaspoon at a time, whisking continuously. Fold in the coconut. Fit a piping bag with a medium star nozzle and fill the bag with the mixture. Pipe nine swirls on to the prepared baking tray or spoon on if you prefer.

Cook in a very cool oven (110°C, 225°F, Gas Mark $\frac{1}{4}$) for 3$\frac{1}{2}$ hours, or until completely dry.

Store in an airtight tin for up to 1 week.

Cherry Meringues

Approximate preparation time: 30 minutes
Cooking time: 3 hours
Makes 7

3 large egg whites
175 g/6 oz castor sugar
175 g/6 oz icing sugar
75 g/3 oz unsalted butter
1 tablespoon lemon juice
50 g/2 oz cocktail cherries

Line two baking trays with foil. Whisk the egg whites until very stiff and standing in peaks. Whisk in the sugar, a teaspoon at a time, whisking continuously. Fit a piping bag with a medium star nozzle and fill the bag with the meringue. Pipe or spoon seven rounds on each prepared baking tray. Cook in a very cool oven (110°C, 225°F, Gas Mark $\frac{1}{4}$) for about 3 hours, or until dry.

Sift the icing sugar and beat in the butter and lemon juice until creamy. Roughly chop the cherries and add to the mixture. Sandwich the meringues together with the mixture and serve the same day.

Store the meringues, unfilled, in an airtight tin for up to 10 days.

Ginger Meringues

Approximate preparation time: 15
minutes
Cooking time: $2\frac{1}{2}$ hours
Makes 7

4 egg whites
225 g/8 oz castor sugar
2 medium oranges
1 (113-g/4-oz) can cream
50 g/2 oz crystallised ginger
angelica for decoration

Line a baking tray with foil or bakewell paper and mark out seven 9-cm/$3\frac{1}{2}$-inch circles.

Whisk the egg whites with half the sugar, adding a teaspoon at a time, until very stiff and standing in peaks. Fold in the remaining sugar with a metal spoon. Fit a piping bag with a medium star nozzle and fill the bag with the meringue. Pipe over the marked circles making a solid base and piping sides to the meringue nests. Cook in a very cool oven (110°C, 225°F, Gas Mark $\frac{1}{4}$) for about $2\frac{1}{2}$ hours, or until dry. Cool on the baking tray.

Peel the oranges and cut in segments. Fill the nests with the cream and add the orange, ginger and angelica. Serve within 3 hours of filling, or the meringue will become soggy.

Store the unfilled meringues in an airtight tin for up to 10 days.

White Cloud Meringues

Approximate preparation time: 20
minutes
Cooking time: 2 hours
Makes 8

**3 egg whites
175 g/6 oz castor sugar
175 g/6 oz icing sugar
75 g/3 oz unsalted butter
few drops pink colouring
almond essence to taste**

Line a large baking tray with bakewell paper or foil. Whisk the egg whites until very stiff and standing in peaks. Whisk in half the sugar and fold in the rest using a metal spoon. Fit a piping bag with a large plain nozzle and fill the bag with the meringue. Pipe 16 large blobs on the prepared baking tray. Cook in a very cool oven (110°C, 225°F, Gas Mark $\frac{1}{4}$) for 2 hours or until dry. The meringues should be white. Leave to cool.

Sift the icing sugar and beat in the butter and colouring until light and creamy. Flavour with almond essence and use to sandwich pairs of meringues together.

Blender Cakes

Approximate preparation time: 20
minutes plus standing time
Cooking time: 15–20 minutes
Makes 6

240 g/8½ oz granulated sugar, plus a
little extra
190 g/6½ oz butter or margarine
grated rind of 1 small orange
1 large egg yolk
100 g/4 oz plain flour
4 tablespoons orange juice
3 glacé cherries

Grease two large baking trays. Place the sugar in the liquidiser and blend until powdery.

Cream 100 g/4 oz of the butter or margarine and beat in 50 g/2 oz of the sugar with the orange rind and egg yolk. Sift the flour and fold into the creamed mixture with a metal spoon. Fit a piping bag with a large star nozzle and fill the bag with the mixture. Pipe 12 rounds on to the prepared baking tray, leaving space around each one. Chill for 30 minutes.

Cook in a moderately hot oven (190°C, 375°F, Gas Mark 5) for 15–20 minutes, then use a palette knife to transfer to a wire rack.

Cream the remaining butter or margarine with 175 g/6 oz of the sugar and the orange juice. Sandwich the rounds together with some of the mixture. Dust the rounds with the remaining sugar. Put a little icing and half a cherry on each cake.

Eat the same day.

Crunchy Caramel Cakes

Approximate preparation time: 25
minutes
Cooking time: 45 minutes
Makes 16

225 g/8 oz butter
150 g/5 oz castor sugar
175 g/6 oz self-raising flour
pinch of salt
1 tablespoon golden syrup
1 (397-g/14-oz) can condensed milk
75 g/3 oz plain chocolate

Rub together half the butter, 25 g/1 oz of the sugar, the flour and salt. Press together to make a dough and press into an 18-cm/7-inch square cake tin. Smooth the top and prick lightly. Cook in a moderate oven (180°C, 350°F, Gas Mark 4) for 35 minutes, or until golden. Cool in the tin.

Put the remaining butter and sugar in a pan with the syrup, condensed milk and 3 tablespoons cold water. Stir over a low heat until the sugar has dissolved. Bring to the boil and boil slowly for 8 minutes or until caramel coloured, stirring all the time. Remove from the heat and beat until it begins to thicken. Pour over the baked base and leave to cool.

Melt the chocolate in a small bowl over a pan of simmering water. Pour over the caramel and decorate using the blade of a knife. Leave to set. Remove and cut into 16 pieces.

Store in an airtight container for up to 1 week.

Rhubarb Shortcakes

Approximate preparation time: 20
minutes
Cooking time: 30 minutes
Makes 8

350 g/12 oz plain flour
1 teaspoon baking powder
75 g/3 oz margarine
50 g/2 oz castor sugar
1 egg
4 tablespoons milk
1 (594-g/1 lb 5-oz) can rhubarb

Lightly grease a shallow 18-cm/7-inch square cake tin.

Sift the flour and baking powder together. Rub in the margarine until the mixture resembles breadcrumbs, then stir in the sugar. Mix the egg and milk and work into the mixture to make a firm dough.

Divide the dough in half and roll out one piece to fit the cake tin. Drain the rhubarb and spoon the fruit over the lined tin. Roll out the second half and place over the rhubarb. Cook in a moderately hot oven (200°C, 400°F, Gas Mark 6) for 30 minutes or until cooked. Leave to cool, then cut into triangles.

This is best eaten the same day. If liked you can use fresh stewed rhubarb for the filling.

Cinnamon Shortcake

Approximate preparation time: 15
minutes
Cooking time: 25–30 minutes
Makes 6

100 g/4 oz butter
100 g/4 oz plain flour
pinch of salt
$\frac{1}{4}$ teaspoon ground cinnamon
65 g/$2\frac{1}{2}$ oz castor sugar

Lightly grease a 20-cm/8-inch plain or fluted flan tin.

Beat the butter until creamy. Mix in the flour, salt, cinnamon and all but 15 g/$\frac{1}{2}$ oz of the sugar. Knead to make a firm dough. Press this into the flan tin and smooth the top. Mark into six segments and prick all over with a fork.

Cook in a moderate oven (180°C, 350°F, Gas Mark 4) for 25–30 minutes. Sprinkle with the remaining sugar.

Cool and cut into pieces.

Store in an airtight tin for up to 2 weeks, or freeze for up to 2 months. Thaw for 4–5 hours.

Chocolate Oatcakes

Approximate preparation time: 20 minutes
Cooking time: 15–20 minutes
Makes 14

50 g/2 oz margarine
50 g/2 oz castor sugar
1 egg
90 g/3½ oz self-raising flour
1 tablespoon cocoa powder
25 g/1 oz porridge oats
7 glacé cherries

Grease a baking tray.

Cream the margarine with the sugar until light and fluffy. Beat the egg and add gradually to the creamed mixture. Sift the flour and cocoa over the mixture and fold in with a metal spoon.

Using damp hands, divide the mixture into 14. Shape each piece into a ball and roll in the oats. Place on the prepared baking tray, leaving space between them. Flatten slightly and press half a cherry into the top of each. Cook in a moderately hot oven (190°C, 375°F, Gas Mark 5) for 15–20 minutes. Cool on a wire rack.

Store for up to 2 days in an airtight tin.

Variation
Instead of the halved cherries, spread a little melted plain chocolate or chocolate cake covering over the cooked oatcakes.

Oat Cookies

Approximate preparation time: 10
minutes
Cooking time: 20 minutes
Makes 12

100 g/4 oz castor sugar
100 g/4 oz butter
100 g/4 oz porridge oats
6 glacé cherries

Oatmeal is very nutritious. This is a good way of ensuring that the children get iron! They will love these little cookies.

Lightly grease two baking trays.

Beat the sugar and butter lightly with a wooden spoon. Mix in the oats. Divide the mixture into 12 and shape into balls. Place six balls on each prepared baking tray, leaving plenty of space around each one. Flatten them a little, then cook in a moderately hot oven (190°C, 375°F, Gas Mark 5) for about 20 minutes, until firm and golden.

Halve the cherries and press on to the warm cookies. When almost cold, lift off the baking trays and leave on a wire rack.

Store in an airtight tin.

Oat Slices

Approximate preparation time: 20
minutes
Cooking time: 30 minutes
Makes 10

225 g/8 oz porridge oats
pinch of salt
150 g/5 oz margarine
1 tablespoon golden syrup
50 g/2 oz demerara sugar
1 tablespoon lemon juice
50 g/2 oz stoned dates, finely
chopped

Lightly grease an 18-cm/7-inch square cake tin and line the base with greaseproof paper.

Mix the oats with the salt. Melt the margarine in a pan with the syrup, sugar and lemon juice. Cool a little.

Stir the dates into the oats, then add the melted mixture. Stir well. Spoon into the prepared tin, smooth the top and cook in a moderately hot oven (190°C, 375°F, Gas Mark 5) for 30 minutes. Cool slightly then cut into fingers, still in the tin. Turn out when cold.

Store for up to 3 days in an airtight tin or wrapped in foil.

Variation
If liked, add a generous pinch of ground ginger to the mixture.

Date Flapjacks

Approximate preparation time: 20
minutes
Cooking time: 30–40 minutes
Makes 8

100 g/4 oz margarine
25 g/1 oz soft brown sugar
3 tablespoons golden syrup
225 g/8 oz porridge oats
pinch of salt
50 g/2 oz dates, chopped
75 g/3 oz icing sugar (optional)

Grease a 19-cm/7$\frac{1}{2}$-inch square tin and line the base with greaseproof paper.

Cream the margarine and sugar together until light and fluffy. Warm the syrup and stir into the creamed mixture. Work in the oats, salt and dates. Place the mixture in the prepared tin and cook in a moderately hot oven (190°C, 375°F, Gas Mark 5) for 30–40 minutes.

Cool in the tin then cut into triangles. If icing the flapjacks, sift the icing sugar and add just enough water to make a coating mixture. Fit a piping bag with a small plain nozzle and fill the bag with the icing. Pipe loops over the top of the flapjacks.

Store for up to 4 days in an airtight tin.

Brandy Snaps

Approximate preparation time: 25
minutes
Cooking time: 15–20 minutes
Makes 8

75 g/3 oz golden syrup
50 g/2 oz castor sugar
75 g/3 oz margarine
50 g/2 oz plain flour
1 teaspoon ground ginger
150 ml/$\frac{1}{4}$ pint whipped cream

Grease a baking tray well.

Melt the syrup, sugar and margarine together. Sift the flour with the ginger. Cool the syrup a little, then pour into the flour. Mix well. Place teaspoons of the mixture about 10-cm/4-inches apart on the prepared baking tray. Bake in a moderately hot oven (190°C, 375°F, Gas Mark 5) for 15–20 minutes, until well spread and golden brown.

Grease the handle of a wooden spoon and, lifting each brandy snap with a palette knife, roll them around the handle and slide off carefully. To soften them, return to the oven. Leave to cool and harden.

Store in an airtight tin for up to 2 weeks. Fill with whipped cream before serving.

Variation

Chocolate Snaps. Make as for brandy snaps but do not fill with cream. Melt 100 g/4 oz chocolate cake covering and dip the ends of the rolled snaps in the chocolate. Leave to set. Ordinary plain chocolate may be used, but it will discolour in 4–5 hours.

Almond Fingers

Approximate preparation time: 20
minutes
Cooking time: 40 minutes
Makes 20

1 (212-g/7$\frac{1}{2}$-oz) packet frozen
shortcrust pastry, thawed
3 tablespoons raspberry jam
2 large egg whites
75 g/3 oz ground almonds
75 g/3 oz castor sugar
few drops almond essence
25 g/1 oz flaked almonds

Grease a 28×18-cm/11×7-inch Swiss roll tin.

Roll out the pastry to just larger than the tin and line the base and sides with it. Spread the jam over the pastry. Whisk the egg whites until very stiff and standing in peaks. Mix the ground almonds and sugar together and fold into the egg whites with the almond essence, using a metal spoon. Spoon over the layer of jam and sprinkle with flaked almonds.

Cook in a moderately hot oven (200°C, 400°F, Gas Mark 6) for about 40 minutes, until well risen and golden. Cool in the tin then turn out and cut in oblongs.

Store for up to 4 days in an airtight tin.

Little Apple Tarts

Approximate preparation time: 25
minutes
Cooking time: 32–37 minutes
Makes 12

175 g/6 oz plain flour
pinch of salt
40 g/1½ oz margarine
40 g/1½ oz lard
175 g/6 oz castor sugar
2 large cooking apples
2 cloves

Lightly grease 12 patty tins.

Sift the flour and salt together. Add the margarine and lard, cut in pieces, and rub in with the fingertips until the mixture resembles breadcrumbs. Stir in 25 g/1 oz of the sugar. Mix in just enough cold water to make a firm dough. Leave in a cool place.

Peel, core and slice the apples. Place in a saucepan with the remaining sugar, the cloves and 2 tablespoons water. Cover and simmer for 5 minutes.

Roll out the pastry on a lightly floured surface and cut in rounds with a plain or fluted cutter. Use these to line the patty tins.

Drain the apples, remove the cloves and allow to cool a little. Spoon the apple into the pastry cases and cook in a moderately hot oven (200°C, 400°F, Gas Mark 6) for 20–25 minutes. Eat the same day.

Variations

If preferred, use a generous teaspoon of grated orange rind in place of the cloves, or decorate with slices of red-skinned apple tossed in lemon juice.

Sunday Tartlets

Approximate preparation time: 35
minutes
Cooking time: 30 minutes
Makes 10

240 g/8½ oz plain flour
115 g/4½ oz castor sugar
2 large eggs plus 1 large egg yolk
115 g/4½ oz margarine
300 ml/½ pint milk
few drops vanilla essence
fresh fruit for filling, cooked if
necessary
5 tablespoons sieved apricot jam

Sift all but 25 g/1 oz of the flour into a bowl, make a well in the centre and add 75 g/3 oz of the sugar, 1 egg, 1 egg yolk and the margarine. Use the fingertips to rub in the ingredients to make a smooth paste. Wrap in greaseproof paper or foil and chill for 30 minutes.

Mix the egg with the remaining sugar and flour. Heat the milk and vanilla essence to simmering point and pour on to the egg mixture. Mix well then return to the pan. Bring to the boil and cook for 1 minute, stirring continuously. Pour into a bowl and cover with clingfilm.

Roll out the pastry and use to line ten large deep tartlet tins. Prick the bases and bake blind in a moderately hot oven (200°C, 400°F, Gas Mark 6) for 20 minutes. Cool. Place a spoonful of the custard in each case and pile the fruit on top. Heat the jam and brush over the tops. Eat the same day.

Tiny Fruit Tartlets

Approximate preparation time: 25
minutes plus standing time
Cooking time: 45 minutes–1 hour
Makes 18

100 g/4 oz plain flour
50 g/2 oz hard margarine
150 ml/$\frac{1}{4}$ pint double cream
2 teaspoons castor sugar
few drops rum essence
225 g/8 oz fresh strawberries or
thawed frozen raspberries

Sift the flour and add the margarine, cut in pieces. Rub in until the mixture resembles breadcrumbs. Add enough cold water to make a stiff dough. Roll the dough out thinly on a lightly floured surface. Cut out 5-cm/2-inch rounds with a small cutter and press into tiny bun tins. Prick the pastry with a fork and chill for 15 minutes.

Bake the tartlets in three batches in a moderately hot oven (200°C, 400°F, Gas Mark 6) for 15–20 minutes each. Leave to cool.

Whip the cream with the sugar until thick. Stir in rum essence to taste. Pipe or spoon into the baked cases and top with the chosen fruit. Eat the same day.

Coconut Boats

Approximate preparation time: 25
minutes plus standing time
Cooking time: 25 minutes
Makes 8

40 g/1$\frac{1}{2}$ oz desiccated coconut
40 g/1$\frac{1}{2}$ oz margarine
40 g/1$\frac{1}{2}$ oz castor sugar
1 egg
25 g/1 oz self-raising flour
1 (212-g/7$\frac{1}{2}$-oz) packet frozen
shortcrust pastry, thawed
2 tablespoons chocolate spread
50 g/2 oz icing sugar
shredded or desiccated coconut
(optional)

Pour 2 tablespoons boiling water over the desiccated coconut. Cream the margarine with the sugar until light and fluffy and gradually beat in the egg. Sift the flour on top, add the soaked coconut and fold in with a metal spoon.

Roll out the pastry and use to line eight boat-shaped or round tartlet tins. Put half the chocolate spread in the lined tins, then cover with the coconut mixture. Place the tins on a baking tray. Bake in a moderately hot oven (190°C, 375°F, Gas Mark 5) for 25 minutes. Cool on a wire rack.

Sift the icing sugar and mix with the remaining chocolate spread and 2 teaspoons hot water. Spread some on each tartlet. Sprinkle with coconut if used.

If using home-made pastry, these can be frozen and stored for up to 6 weeks. Thaw for 4–5 hours. These cakes are perfect for packed lunches.

Little Chocolate Tarts

Approximate preparation time: 25 minutes
Cooking time: 20 minutes
Makes 12

1 (212-g/7½-oz) packet frozen
shortcrust pastry, thawed
50 g/2 oz self-raising flour
15 g/½ oz cocoa powder
50 g/2 oz margarine
50 g/2 oz castor sugar
1 large egg
2 tablespoons raspberry jam

Roll out the pastry on a lightly floured surface and cut out 12 (7.5-cm/3-inch) rounds using a plain or fluted cutter. Use the rounds to fill 12 patty tins.

Sift the flour and cocoa together and add the margarine, cut in pieces, the sugar and egg. Beat for 2 minutes or until smooth using a wooden spoon.

Spoon a little jam into each pastry case and spoon the chocolate mixture on top. Bake in a moderately hot oven (200°C, 400°F, Gas Mark 6) for 20 minutes. Cool on a wire rack.

These tarts may be frozen if made with home-made pastry. Store for up to 6 weeks. Thaw for 4–5 hours.

Marmalade Tarts

Approximate preparation time: 20 minutes
Cooking time: 20 minutes
Makes 12

1 (212-g/7½-oz) packet frozen
shortcrust pastry, thawed
65 g/2½ oz self-raising flour
50 g/2 oz soft margarine
50 g/2 oz castor sugar
1 large egg
1 tablespoon coarse-cut marmalade
shredded orange rind (optional)

Roll out the pastry on a lightly floured surface and cut out 12 rounds with a 7.5-cm/3-inch fluted cutter. Use these rounds to line 12 patty tins.

Sift the flour into a bowl, add the margarine, cut in pieces, with the sugar and egg. Beat for 2 minutes then beat in the marmalade. Divide the mixture between the pastry cases and bake in a moderately hot oven (200°C, 400°F, Gas Mark 6) for 20 minutes or until golden. Cool on a wire rack then sprinkle with shredded orange rind if liked. These tarts are best eaten fresh and warm.

If using home-made pastry, these tarts may be frozen for up to 2 months. Thaw for 4–5 hours.

Apricot Pastry Cakes

Approximate preparation time: 25
minutes
Cooking time: 30 minutes
Makes 14

1 (212-g/7½-oz) packet frozen puff
pastry, thawed
100 g/4 oz margarine
100 g/4 oz castor sugar
3 drops almond essence
2 large eggs
100 g/4 oz self-raising flour
4 tablespoons apricot jam, sieved

Roll out the pastry on a lightly floured surface and cut out rounds to line 14 brioche or deep tartlet tins. Place on a baking tray. Chill while making the filling.

Cream the margarine and sugar with the almond essence until light and fluffy. Gradually beat in the eggs. Sift the flour and fold into the mixture using a metal spoon.

Divide half the jam between the pastry cases and spoon the cake mixture on top. Cook in a hot oven (220°C, 425°F. Gas Mark 7) for 10 minutes then reduce to moderate (180°C, 350°F, Gas Mark 4) and cook for a further 20 minutes. Cool on a wire rack. Heat the remaining jam with 1 tablespoon water and brush over the cooked cakes. Eat the same day.

Spicy Triangles

Approximate preparation time: 20
minutes
Cooking time: 25 minutes
Makes 12

75 g/3 oz Madeira cake
40 g/1½ oz butter
40 g/1½ oz castor sugar
75 g/3 oz mixed dried fruit
¼ teaspoon ground mixed spice
pinch of grated nutmeg
1 (370-g/13-oz) packet frozen puff
pastry, thawed
2 tablespoons milk

Rub the cake through a sieve or put in a liquidiser to make crumbs.

Melt the butter in a saucepan and remove from the heat. Stir in 25 g/1 oz of the sugar, the crumbs, dried fruit, spice and nutmeg. Leave to cool.

Roll out the pastry on a floured surface to a 30 × 42-cm/12 × 16-inch rectangle. Cut into 12 squares. Divide the fruit mixture between the squares. Brush the pastry edges with water and fold over to make triangles, sealing the edges. Brush the tops with milk and sprinkle with the remaining sugar. Make three cuts on top of each triangle, place on a dampened baking tray and cook in a hot oven (220°C, 425°F, Gas Mark 7) for 25 minutes. Cool on a wire rack. Eat fresh.

Variation
If liked, use finely chopped or minced dates in the filling instead of dried fruit.

Date Pastries

Approximate preparation time: 20
minutes
Cooking time: 20 minutes
Makes 8

75 g/3 oz chopped dates
25 g/1 oz sultanas
1 tablespoon golden syrup
1 (370-g/13-oz) packet frozen puff
pastry, thawed
15 g/$\frac{1}{2}$ oz castor sugar

If your family don't like dates you could use
a mixture of chopped raw banana (a small
ripe one) and sultanas, or banana and
chopped soaked dried apricots instead.

Finely chop the dates and mix with the
sultanas and syrup. Roll out the pastry on a
lightly floured surface and cut out eight
rounds, using a small plate or saucer as a
guide.

Divide the date mixture between the
rounds, leaving the edges clear. Damp the
edges and fold over so the filling is sealed in.
Brush the pastries with water and sprinkle
with the sugar. Place on a dampened baking
tray and cook in a hot oven (220°C, 425°F,
Gas Mark 7) for 20 minutes, or until golden.
Cool on a wire rack. Eat the same day.

If home-made pastry is used, these pastries can be frozen and stored for up to 2
months.

Plum Pastries

Approximate preparation time: 10
minutes
Cooking time: 15 minutes
Makes 7

1 (212-g/7$\frac{1}{2}$-oz) packet frozen puff
pastry, thawed
1 small egg yolk
4 tablespoons plum jam
1 tablespoon icing sugar

Roll out the pastry on a lightly floured board
to 5-mm/$\frac{1}{4}$-inch thick. Cut out seven rounds
using a 7.5-cm/3-inch cutter. Place on a
dampened baking tray and make a criss-
cross pattern on top using a sharp knife.
Beat the egg yolk and brush over the pastry.
Bake in a hot oven (220°C, 425°F, Gas Mark
7) for 15 minutes until well risen.

Cool on a wire rack, then split horizontally
and sandwich back together with the jam.
Sift the icing sugar over the tops. Eat the
same day.

Variation
Use any other flavours of jam such as
blackcurrant or gooseberry for a change.
These alternatives give a good sharp taste.

Raspberry Palmiers

Approximate preparation time: 10
minutes
Cooking time: 20 minutes
Makes 4–6

50 g/2 oz plus 2 tablespoons castor
sugar
1 (212-g/7½-oz) packet frozen puff
pastry, thawed
150 ml/¼ pint double cream
few drops vanilla essence
100 g/4 oz thawed frozen
raspberries or raspberry jam

Sprinkle some of the sugar on a pastry board. Place the pastry on the sugar and sprinkle more on top. Roll out to a 30 × 10-cm/12 × 4-inch oblong. Sprinkle with sugar. Fold the top third of the pastry down and the bottom third up to give three thicknesses of pastry. Give the pastry a quarter turn so that the folded edges are at the sides. Sprinkle with sugar and roll out to larger than before. Fold the short sides into the middle and press. Sprinkle with sugar and bring the folded sides to the centre again. Fold once to make a long strip. Press together and cut into 5-mm/¼-inch slices.

Place the slices flat on a baking tray and cook in a hot oven (220°C, 425°F, Gas Mark 7) for 10 minutes. Turn over and cook for a further 10 minutes. Whip the cream with the vanilla and remaining sugar. Fold the fruit or jam into the cream and use to sandwich the palmiers.

Grape Horns

Approximate preparation time: 30
minutes
Cooking time: 15–20 minutes
Makes 6

1 (212-g/7½-oz) packet frozen
puff pastry, thawed
1 small egg yolk
3 tablespoons pineapple jam
150 ml/¼ pint whipped cream
175 g/6 oz small green grapes,
washed and dried

Damp a baking tray and grease six metal cream horn tins.

Roll out the pastry on a lightly floured surface to a thin oblong. Cut in six even strips. Damp these slightly on one side.

With the damp side next to the tin, starting at the pointed end, wind the pastry around the horn tins, overlapping and sealing with beaten egg as you go. Brush all over with egg yolk to glaze.

Bake in a hot oven (230°C, 450°F, Gas Mark 8) for 12–15 minutes. Remove the tins and allow to cool. Fill with the jam. Mix the cream and grapes together and spoon into the horns. Serve as soon as possible. These look really special if served on a white doily – they also make good buffet fare as they are easy to pick up.

Variations
When raspberries are in season, use these instead of grapes, or use very small ripe strawberries or blackberries.

For a cheaper teatime treat, use all jam in place of cream and fruit. Apricot, pineapple or strawberry would be best and give a good colour.

FAMILY CAKES

Banana and Honey Teabread

Approximate preparation time: 20 minutes
Cooking time: 1 hour 5 minutes

275 g/10 oz plain flour
pinch of grated nutmeg
150 g/5 oz castor sugar
3 teaspoons baking powder
75 g/3 oz clear honey
75 g/3 oz margarine
2 medium bananas
75 g/3 oz icing sugar
grated rind and juice of 1 small
lemon

Lightly grease a 0.5-kg/1-lb loaf tin.

Sift the flour, nutmeg, sugar and baking powder into a bowl. Make a well in the centre.

Put the honey and margarine in a saucepan with 150 ml/$\frac{1}{4}$ pint water. Stir until the fat has melted, then set aside to cool a little.

Peel one and a half bananas and mash with a fork. Stir this into the melted mixture. Pour into the flour and stir until evenly mixed, using a wooden spoon. Pour into the prepared tin and cook in a moderate oven (180°C, 350°F, Gas Mark 4) for 1 hour 5 minutes. Turn out and cool on a wire rack.

Sift the icing sugar and add enough lemon juice to make a thick icing. Stir in the rind and pour over the cooled cake. Slice the remaining banana and arrange on the top. Serve in slices, spread with butter.

Store in an airtight tin and eat within 2 days.

Syrup and Orange Loaf

Approximate preparation time: 15 minutes
Cooking time: 1 hour 10 minutes

350 g/12 oz plain flour
1 teaspoon bicarbonate of soda
$\frac{1}{2}$ teaspoon ground cinnamon
100 g/4 oz margarine or butter
100 g/4 oz castor sugar
grated rind and juice of 1 small
orange
75 g/3 oz chopped mixed peel
2 tablespoons golden syrup
4 tablespoons milk

Lightly grease a 0.75-kg/1$\frac{1}{2}$-lb loaf tin and line the base with greaseproof paper.

Sift the flour with the bicarbonate of soda and cinnamon. Rub in the margarine or butter until the mixture resembles fine breadcrumbs. Stir in the sugar, orange rind and two-thirds of the peel.

Put the orange juice in a small saucepan with the syrup and heat gently. Stir into the dry ingredients. Add the milk and mix until smooth. Turn into the prepared tin and cook in a moderate oven (180°C, 350°F, Gas Mark 4) for 1 hour 5 minutes. Sprinkle the remaining peel over the loaf.

Store in an airtight tin and eat within 2 days.

Variation
For extra decoration, spoon a little glacé icing on before adding the peel.

Pear Loaf

Approximate preparation time: 20 minutes
Cooking time: 55 minutes

225 g/8 oz self-raising flour
$\frac{1}{4}$ teaspoon ground mixed spice
100 g/4 oz castor sugar
100 g/4 oz margarine
1 medium dessert pear
1 egg
3 tablespoons milk
15 g/$\frac{1}{2}$ oz icing sugar

Lightly grease a 0.75-kg/1$\frac{1}{2}$-lb loaf tin and line the base with greaseproof paper.

Sift the flour and spice into a bowl and stir in the sugar. Rub in the margarine until the mixture resembles fine breadcrumbs. Peel, core and finely chop the pear and stir into the dry mixture. Beat the egg with the milk and mix with the dry ingredients to make a stiff dough. Turn into the prepared tin, smooth the top and bake in a moderate oven (180°C, 350°F, Gas Mark 4) for 55 minutes or until cooked. Cool on a wire rack then sift icing sugar over the top.

Don't try to use tinned pears for this recipe, they won't be successful; they are too soft and don't have nearly enough flavour.

Store for up to 2 days in an airtight tin.

Date and Apple Loaf

Approximate preparation time: 25 minutes
Cooking time: 1 hour 10 minutes

175 g/6 oz self-raising flour
75 g/3 oz margarine
75 g/3 oz castor sugar
50 g/2 oz chopped dates
1 medium cooking apple
1 large egg
2$\frac{1}{2}$ tablespoons milk
1 tablespoon golden syrup
50 g/2 oz icing sugar

Lightly grease a 0.75-kg/1$\frac{1}{2}$-lb loaf tin and line the base with greaseproof paper.

Sift the flour and rub in 50 g/2 oz of the margarine until the mixture resembles fine breadcrumbs. Stir in the sugar and dates.

Peel and core the apple. Cut half in slices and chop the rest. Add the chopped apple to the mixture. Beat the egg and add to the mixture with enough milk to make a stiff dough. Turn into the prepared tin and arrange the sliced apple overlapping down the centre. Cook in a moderately hot oven (190°C, 375°F, Gas Mark 5) for about 1 hour 10 minutes. Cool on a wire rack.

Spoon the syrup over the top. Sift the icing sugar and beat in the remaining margarine and about 2 teaspoons milk. Fit a piping bag with a small star nozzle and fill the bag with the mixture. Pipe around the edge of the cake.

Freeze the cake without the decoration. Store for up to 2 months. Thaw for 4–5 hours.

Prune Loaf

Approximate preparation time: 15
minutes plus standing time
Cooking time: $1\frac{1}{4}$–$1\frac{1}{2}$ hours

100 g/4 oz prunes, chopped
100 g/4 oz porridge oats
grated rind of $\frac{1}{2}$ small lemon
100 g/4 oz butter
75 g/3 oz soft brown sugar
1 large egg
175 g/6 oz plain flour
$1\frac{1}{2}$ teaspoons bicarbonate of soda
$1\frac{1}{2}$ teaspoons ground cinnamon
$\frac{1}{4}$ teaspoon ground cloves
$\frac{1}{4}$ teaspoon salt

Put the prunes and oats in a bowl and pour on 300 ml/$\frac{1}{2}$ pint boiling water. Stir in the lemon rind and leave to stand for 20 minutes.

Grease a 15-cm/6-inch square cake tin and line the base with greaseproof paper.

Cream the butter and sugar together until light and fluffy. Beat the egg and add gradually to the creamed mixture. Sift the flour with the bicarbonate of soda, cinnamon, cloves and salt. Fold into the creamed mixture with a metal spoon. Fold in the prune mixture in the same way. Turn into the prepared tin and cook in a moderate oven (180°C, 350°F, Gas Mark 4) for $1\frac{1}{4}$–$1\frac{1}{2}$ hours. Turn out and cool on a wire rack. Serve in slices with butter.

Variation
For extra flavour, add 2 tablespoons sweet or medium sherry to the soaking mixture in place of the same amount of boiling water.

Fruity Syrup Loaf

Approximate preparation time: 15
minutes
Cooking time: 1 hour

225 g/8 oz self-raising flour
50 g/2 oz plus 2 teaspoons malted
milk drink powder
100 g/4 oz mixed dried fruit
25 g/1 oz chopped mixed peel
50 g/2 oz castor sugar
4 tablespoons golden syrup
150 ml/$\frac{1}{4}$ pint milk

Grease and flour a 0.5-kg/1-lb loaf tin.

Sift the flour into a bowl and add the 50 g/2 oz Ovaltine, the fruit, peel and sugar. Put $2\frac{1}{2}$ tablespoons of the syrup in a saucepan with the milk and heat until the syrup just melts. Pour into the flour and stir until well mixed. Turn into the prepared tin and cook in a moderate oven (180°C, 350°F, Gas Mark 4) for about 1 hour, or until firm. Turn out and cool on a wire rack.

Brush the top of the loaf with the remaining syrup and dust with the Ovaltine. Eat the same day when at its moistest. Serve sliced with butter.

Store in an airtight container.

Variation
For the cake itself, use 1 tablespoon treacle in place of the same amount of syrup. Still use syrup to glaze the top.

Teatime Loaf

Approximate preparation time: 15
minutes
Cooking time: 1 hour

75 g/3 oz margarine
100 g/4 oz castor sugar
2 eggs
75 g/3 oz currants
225 g/8 oz plain flour
pinch of salt
1 teaspoon baking powder
pinch of grated nutmeg
2 tablespoons milk

Grease a 0.5-kg/1-lb loaf tin and line the
base with greaseproof paper.

Cream the margarine and sugar until light
and fluffy. Beat the eggs and add gradually.
Stir in the currants.

Sift the flour with the salt, baking powder
and nutmeg and fold into the creamed
mixture using a metal spoon. Stir in the milk
and turn into the prepared tin. Cook in a
moderate oven (180°C, 350°F, Gas Mark 4)
for about 1 hour or until firm. Eat the same
day if possible.

This loaf may be frozen. Store for up to 2
months. Thaw for 4–5 hours.

Freezer packing
*'Solid' cakes, those with no decoration or
topping which might spoil, can be wrapped in foil for freezing. Otherwise you must
always put them into a plastic box with a
lid, being careful to leave room at the top to
prevent damage to the cake!*

Country Loaf

Approximate preparation time: 15
minutes
Cooking time: 1 hour 10 minutes

225 g/8 oz plain flour
$\frac{1}{4}$ teaspoon salt
1 teaspoon ground mixed spice
100 g/4 oz lard
100 g/4 oz soft brown sugar
50 g/2 oz currants
75 g/3 oz sultanas
1 teaspoon bicarbonate of soda
4 tablespoons milk
1 small egg

Grease a 0.75-kg/1$\frac{1}{2}$-lb loaf tin and line the
base with greaseproof paper.

Sift the flour, salt and spice into a bowl.
Cut the lard in pieces, add to the flour and
rub in with the fingertips until the mixture
resembles fine breadcrumbs. Stir in the
sugar, currants and sultanas. Dissolve the
bicarbonate of soda in the milk, add the egg
and beat into the mixture. Turn into the
prepared tin and cook in a moderate oven
(180°C, 350°F, Gas Mark 4) for 1 hour 10
minutes, or until firm.

Store in an airtight tin and eat within 2
days.

Variations
If you like, use granulated sugar, add
150 g/5 oz chopped dates instead of the
sultanas and currants, or add a little vanilla
essence.

Orange Lardy Cake

Approximate preparation time: 25
minutes plus rising time
Cooking time: 45–50 minutes

450 g/1 lb plain flour
$\frac{1}{2}$ teaspoon salt
50 g/2 oz margarine
grated rind of 1 small orange
2 teaspoons dried yeast
100 g/4 oz castor sugar
75 g/3 oz lard
75 g/3 oz currants
$\frac{1}{2}$ teaspoon ground mixed spice
2 tablespoons golden syrup
1 orange (optional)

Sift the flour and salt into a bowl. Cut the margarine in pieces and rub in with the fingertips. Stir in the orange rind.

Sprinkle the yeast over 300 ml/$\frac{1}{2}$ pint warm water with 1 teaspoon of the sugar and leave for 10 minutes until frothy. Make a well in the flour and pour in the yeast liquid. Add half the sugar and mix well. Knead until smooth. Put in a large, oiled polythene bag and leave in a warm place until the dough has doubled in size, about 1 hour.

Grease a deep 18-cm/7-inch square cake tin.

Turn out the dough and knead lightly. Roll out to a 30×35-cm/12×14-inch oblong. Cut half the lard in small pieces and dot over two-thirds of the dough. Mix the remaining sugar with the currants and spice and sprinkle half over the larded two-thirds. Fold the uncovered third of dough down and the other third up. Give the dough a quarter turn. Roll out, dot with lard and sprinkle with sugar and fruit as before. Fold up in the same way. Give a quarter turn and roll and fold again. Put in the prepared tin and leave for 15 minutes. Spoon the syrup over the top and cook in a hot oven (220°C, 425°F, Gas Mark 7) for 45–50 minutes. Turn out and decorate with slices of orange if liked.

Eat the same day. You can freeze this cake; store for up to 2 months and thaw for 4–5 hours.

Simnel Cake

Approximate preparation time: 40
minutes plus overnight standing
Cooking time: 2–2$\frac{1}{2}$ hours

175 g/6 oz margarine
175 g/6 oz soft brown sugar
3 large eggs
225 g/8 oz plain flour
$\frac{1}{2}$ teaspoon baking powder
3 teaspoons ground mixed spice
100 g/4 oz sultanas
100 g/4 oz raisins
50 g/2 oz glacé cherries, halved
50 g/2 oz blanched almonds, chopped
50 g/2 oz chopped mixed peel
350 g/12 oz marzipan
2 tablespoons apricot jam, heated and sieved
1 small egg white

Grease an 18-cm/7-inch round cake tin and line with greaseproof paper.

Cream the margarine with the sugar until light and fluffy. Beat the eggs and add gradually to the creamed mixture. Sift the flour, baking powder and spice over the top and fold in with a metal spoon. Stir in the sultanas, raisins, cherries, almonds and peel. Put half the mixture into the prepared tin and spread evenly. Roll out one-third of the marzipan to an 18-cm/7-inch diameter circle and place on the mixture in the tin. Spread the rest of the cake mixture on top. Cook in a moderate oven (160°C, 325°F, Gas Mark·3) for 2–2$\frac{1}{2}$ hours. Leave to cool overnight in the tin.

Turn out and brush the top with apricot jam. Roll half the remaining marzipan to an 18-cm/7-inch diameter circle and place on the cake. Use the remaining marzipan to make eleven balls. Beat the egg white lightly and use to stick the balls around the edge of the cake. Brush the marzipan with egg white and grill for a few seconds until golden.

This cake keeps well; there is no need to freeze. It is best if allowed to mature. Wrap in greaseproof paper and foil and store for 6 weeks before eating. Without the marzipan balls it is suitable for Christmas.

Lemon Sultana Cake

Approximate preparation time: 20 minutes
Cooking time: 50 minutes

175 g/6 oz margarine
175 g/6 oz castor sugar
3 eggs
grated rind and juice of 1 small lemon
200 g/7 oz self-raising flour
50 g/2 oz sultanas
15 g/$\frac{1}{2}$ oz icing sugar

Lightly grease a 15 × 20-cm/6 × 8-inch cake tin and line the base with greaseproof paper.

Cream the margarine and sugar until light and fluffy. Beat the eggs and add gradually to the creamed mixture. Stir in the lemon rind and juice. Sift the flour over the top and fold in with the sultanas. Turn the mixture into the prepared tin and cook in a moderately hot oven (190°C, 375°F, Gas Mark 5) for about 50 minutes. Turn out and cool on a wire rack. Sift the icing sugar over the top.

Eat within 2 days.

Variation

Instead of the icing sugar, make some lemon glacé icing with lemon juice and icing sugar and dribble it over the top.

Sultana Square

Approximate preparation time: 15 minutes
Cooking time: 1 hour 20 minutes – 1 hour 30 minutes

350 g/12 oz self-raising flour
pinch of salt
175 g/6 oz margarine
75 g/3 oz soft brown sugar
75 g/3 oz granulated sugar
75 g/3 oz sultanas
2 eggs
4 tablespoons milk

Lightly grease a 15-cm/6-inch square cake tin and line the base with greaseproof paper.

Sift the flour and salt into a bowl and rub in the margarine until the mixture resembles fine breadcrumbs. Stir in the brown and granulated sugars and the sultanas. Beat the eggs and add to the rubbed-in mixture with enough milk to make a stiff dough. Turn into the prepared cake tin and cook in a moderate oven (180°C, 350°F, Gas Mark 4) for 1 hour 20 minutes – 1 hour 30 minutes. Leave to cool before turning out.

This cake may be frozen. Store for up to 2 months and thaw for 4–5 hours.

Variation

Instead of sultanas, use finely chopped dates. Dates for this can be bought in economical compressed packs.

Sultana Almond Cake

Approximate preparation time: 15 minutes
Cooking time: 35 minutes

100 g/4 oz margarine
100 g/4 oz castor sugar
2 eggs, separated
few drops almond essence
25 g/1 oz sultanas
100 g/4 oz self-raising flour
15 g/$1\frac{1}{2}$ oz flaked almonds
1 teaspoon icing sugar

Lightly grease a 19-cm/$7\frac{1}{2}$-inch sandwich tin and line the base with greaseproof paper.

Cream the margarine with the sugar until light and fluffy. Beat in the egg yolks and almond essence. Stir in the sultanas. Whisk the egg whites until stiff then fold into the mixture with a metal spoon. Sift the flour on top and fold in.

Turn into the prepared cake tin and sprinkle the almonds on top. Cook in a moderately hot oven (190°C, 375°F, Gas Mark 5) for about 35 minutes. Turn out and cool on a wire rack. Sift the icing sugar over the top.

This cake may be frozen. Store for up to 2 months. Thaw for 4–5 hours.

Lining cake tins

Non-stick tins do not need to be lined with greaseproof paper. With other tins, grease the base (and sometimes the sides) with melted lard. Add a round of paper and use a strip of paper to line the sides if needed.

Mincemeat and Lemon Cake

Approximate preparation time: 15 minutes
Cooking time: 1 hour 10 minutes – 1 hour 15 minutes

450 g/1 lb self-raising flour
pinch of salt
175 g/6 oz margarine
175 g/6 oz castor sugar
175 g/6 oz mincemeat
grated rind and juice of 1 small lemon
3 eggs
3 tablespoons milk
15 g/$\frac{1}{2}$ oz granulated sugar

Lightly grease a deep 18-cm/7-inch round cake tin and line the base with greaseproof paper.

Sift the flour and salt into a bowl. Rub in the margarine with the fingertips until the mixture resembles fine breadcrumbs. Stir in the sugar and mincemeat. Mix well with the lemon rind and juice. Beat the eggs with the milk and add to the mixture. Turn into the prepared tin and smooth the top. Cook in a moderate oven (180°C, 350°F, Gas Mark 4) for 1 hour 10 – 1 hour 15 minutes.

Turn out and cool on a wire rack. Sprinkle with granulated sugar when cool.

This cake can be frozen. Store for up to 2 months. Thaw for 4–5 hours.

Date and Coconut Cake

Approximate preparation time: 20 minutes
Cooking time: $1\frac{3}{4}$ hours

150 g/5 oz self-raising flour
25 g/1 oz desiccated coconut
50 g/2 oz dates
50 g/2 oz margarine
25 g/1 oz lard
75 g/3 oz castor sugar
1 small apple
2 eggs

Lightly grease a 15-cm/6-inch round cake tin and line the base and sides with grease-proof paper.

Sift the flour into a bowl. Stir in the coconut. Chop the dates and mix into the flour. Cut the margarine and lard into pieces and rub into the dry ingredients using the fingertips until the mixture resembles fine breadcrumbs. Stir in the sugar. Peel and core the apple. Chop half and add to the mixture. Beat the eggs and add to the mixture. Turn into the prepared tin and smooth the top evenly. Slice the remaining half of apple and arrange the slices on the cake mixture. Cook in a moderate oven (180°C, 350°F, Gas Mark 4) for about $1\frac{3}{4}$ hours.

Eat within 4 days.

Variation
Sultanas or raisins may be substituted for dates if liked.

Plain Apple Cake

Approximate preparation time: 20 minutes
Cooking time: 50 minutes

225 g/8 oz self-raising flour
pinch of salt
25 g/1 oz porridge oats
200 g/7 oz granulated sugar
75 g/3 oz margarine
5 tablespoons milk
1 egg
450 g/1 lb cooking apples

Lightly grease a baking tray and an 18-cm/7-inch fluted or plain flan ring. Stand the ring on the baking tray.

Sift the flour and salt into a bowl. Stir in the oats and 75 g/3 oz of the sugar. Cut the margarine in pieces and rub into the flour until the mixture resembles breadcrumbs. Beat 4 tablespoons of the milk with the egg and add to the mixture to make a soft but not sticky dough. Reserve a small piece of dough. Roll out the rest and fit into the flan ring. Roll out the reserved dough and cut out 2.5-cm/1-inch rounds with a fluted cutter. Arrange these over the dough in the ring. Brush the top with the remaining milk and cook in a hot oven (220°C, 425°F, Gas Mark 7) for 30 minutes. Remove the flan ring and cook for a further 5 minutes. If the cake is getting too brown cover it with a piece of foil. Leave the cooked cake to cool.

Peel, core and slice the apples. Put in a saucepan with the remaining sugar and 2 tablespoons water. Cover and simmer for 15 minutes. Drain and cool. Cut the cake through the middle and sandwich back together with the apple.

To enjoy the cake at its best, eat the same day.

The unfilled cake can be frozen and stored for up to 2 months. Thaw for 4–5 hours.

Citic Cake

Approximate preparation time: 20 minutes
Cooking time: $1\frac{1}{4}$ hours

225 g/8 oz self-raising flour
pinch of salt
100 g/4 oz margarine
100 g/4 oz castor sugar
grated rind and juice of 1 small orange
100 g/4 oz sultanas
1 large egg
2 tablespoons milk
few slices of orange for decoration

Lightly grease a deep 16.5-cm/$6\frac{1}{2}$-inch round cake tin and line the base and sides with greaseproof paper.

Sift the flour and salt into a bowl. Cut the margarine in pieces and rub in until the mixture resembles fine breadcrumbs. Stir in the sugar and orange rind and juice. Mix in the sultanas, egg and milk. Turn into the prepared tin and smooth the top. Cook in a moderate oven (180°C, 350°F, Gas Mark 4) for about $1\frac{1}{4}$ hours or until firm. Turn out and cool on a wire rack. Place the orange slices on the top when the cake is cool.

This cake may be frozen without the decoration for up to 2 months. Defrost for 4–5 hours.

Banana Sponge

Approximate preparation time: 15 minutes
Cooking time: 25–30 minutes

75 g/3 oz margarine
75 g/3 oz castor sugar
1 medium banana
2 tablespoons lemon juice
1 large egg
100 g/4 oz self-raising flour

Lightly grease a 19-cm/$7\frac{1}{2}$-inch sandwich tin and line the base with greaseproof paper.

Cream the margarine and sugar together until light and fluffy. Peel the banana, slice half of it and toss the slices in the lemon juice. Mash the other half and beat into the creamed mixture with the egg. Sift the flour over the top and fold in with a metal spoon. Turn the mixture into the prepared tin and smooth the top. Arrange the slices of banana over the top and cook in a moderately hot oven (200°C, 400°F, Gas Mark 6) for 25–30 minutes. Turn out and cool on a wire rack.

Store in an airtight tin and eat within 3 days.

Orange Coconut Cake

Approximate preparation time: 20 minutes
Cooking time: 30 minutes

100 g/4 oz margarine
100 g/4 oz castor sugar
2 eggs
grated rind and juice of 1 small orange
25 g/1 oz desiccated coconut
100 g/4 oz self-raising flour

Lightly grease a 19-cm/$7\frac{1}{2}$-inch sandwich tin and line the base with greaseproof paper.

Cream the margarine and sugar together until light and fluffy. Beat the eggs and add gradually to the creamed mixture with the orange rind and juice.

Fold in a quarter of the coconut. Sift the flour over the top and fold in with a metal spoon. Turn into the prepared tin, smooth the top and sprinkle with the remaining coconut. Cook in a moderately hot oven (190°C, 375°F, Gas Mark 5) for about 30 minutes. Turn out and cool on a wire rack.

This cake may be frozen. Store for up to 2 months. Thaw for 4–5 hours.

Crushed Pineapple Cake

Approximate preparation time: 25 minutes
Cooking time: 1 hour 20 minutes

225 g/8 oz self-raising flour
2 teaspoons ground ginger
100 g/4 oz butter or margarine
100 g/4 oz granulated sugar
1 large egg
5 tablespoons milk
1 (376-g/13¼-oz) can crushed pineapple
1 teaspoon arrowroot

Grease a deep 15-cm/6-inch round cake tin and line the base and sides with greaseproof paper.

Sift the flour and ginger into a bowl. Cut the butter or margarine in pieces and rub into the flour using the fingertips, until the mixture resembles fine breadcrumbs. Stir in the sugar. Beat the egg with the milk and stir into the rubbed-in mixture, with 2 tablespoons of the pineapple. Turn into the prepared tin and smooth the top. Cook in a moderate oven (180°C, 350°F, Gas Mark 4) for about 1¼ hours. Leave to cool.

Put the remaining pineapple in a saucepan, mixing a little of the juice with the arrowroot until smooth. Add this to the pineapple and bring to the boil, stirring all the time. Boil for 1 minute then spoon over the cake.

This cake may be frozen, but do not wrap in foil because of the acid in the fruit. Use a plastic box. Store for up to 2 months and thaw for 4–5 hours.

Variation
A can of apricots can be used instead of the pineapple. Chop the fruit finely and use in the same way.

Marmalade and Caramel Cake

Approximate preparation time: 20 minutes
Cooking time: 25 minutes

100 g/4 oz margarine
100 g/4 oz castor sugar
2 large eggs
90 g/3½ oz self-raising flour
15 g/½ oz cocoa powder
75 g/3 oz granulated sugar
5 tablespoons marmalade

Lightly grease two 16.5-cm/6½-inch sandwich tins and line the bases with greaseproof paper.

Cream the margarine with the sugar until light and fluffy. Beat the eggs and gradually add to the creamed mixture. Divide the mixture in half and sift 50 g/2 oz of the flour over one half. Fold in with a metal spoon. Sift the remaining flour and the cocoa over the other half and fold in in the same way. Spoon half the plain mixture into one tin and cover with half the cocoa mixture. Put the remaining cocoa mixture in the other tin and spread the plain mixture on top. Cook in a moderately hot oven (190°C, 375°F, Gas Mark 5) for 25 minutes. Turn out and cool on a wire-rack.

To make the caramel, dissolve the sugar in 3 tablespoons water then boil until golden. Leave to cool then crack into pieces. Sandwich the cakes together with the marmalade and sprinkle the caramel on top.

This cake may be frozen without the filling and decoration for up to 2 months. Thaw for 4–5 hours.

Marble Cake

Approximate preparation time: 15 minutes
Cooking time: 1–1¼ hours

2 tablespoons cocoa powder
100 g/4 oz margarine
150 g/5 oz castor sugar
2 eggs
225 g/8 oz self-raising flour
grated rind of 1 small lemon
2 tablespoons milk
1 tablespoon icing sugar

Grease a deep 15-cm/6-inch round cake tin and line the base and sides with greaseproof paper.

Mix the cocoa with 2 tablespoons boiling water and set aside to cool. Cream the margarine and sugar until light and fluffy. Beat the eggs and add gradually to the creamed mixture. Sift the flour over the top and fold in with a metal spoon. Divide the mixture in half. Add the cocoa to one half and the lemon rind and milk to the other. Put alternate spoonfuls of the mixture in the prepared tin. Cook in a moderate oven (180°C, 350°F, Gas Mark 4) for 1–1¼ hours or until firm. Turn out and cool on a wire rack. Sift the icing sugar over the top.

This cake may be frozen for up to 2 months. Thaw for 4–5 hours.

Orange Cake

Approximate preparation time: 25
minutes
Cooking time: 20–25 minutes

100 g/4 oz margarine
100 g/4 oz castor sugar
2 large eggs
100 g/4 oz self-raising flour
grated rind of 1 small orange
150 ml/$\frac{1}{4}$ pint double cream
2 tablespoons marmalade
1–2 tablespoons whisky

Grease two 18-cm/7-inch sandwich tins
and line the bases with greaseproof paper.

Cream the margarine with the sugar until
light and fluffy. Beat the eggs and gradually
add to the creamed mixture. Sift the flour
over the top and fold in with the orange rind,
using a metal spoon. Divide between the
prepared tins, smooth the tops and cook in a
moderately hot oven (190°C, 375°F, Gas
Mark 5) for 20–25 minutes. Turn out and
cool on a wire rack.

Whisk the cream until stiff and use to
sandwich the cakes together. Mix the marmalade with the whisky and spread over the
top.

This freezes very well without the topping. Pack in a plastic box and store for up
to 2 months. Thaw for 4–5 hours and top as
above.

Ginger and Lemon Square

Approximate preparation time: 30 minutes
Cooking time: 1 hour 10 minutes

350 g/12 oz self-raising flour
pinch of salt
1½ teaspoons ground ginger
½ teaspoon ground mixed spice
200 g/7 oz unsalted butter
100 g/4 oz soft brown sugar
6 tablespoons lemon squash
2 large eggs
100 g/4 oz golden syrup
175 g/6 oz icing sugar
100 g/4 oz marzipan

Grease an 18-cm/7-inch square cake tin and line the base and sides with greaseproof paper.

Sift the flour with the salt, ginger and spice. Cut 100 g/4 oz of the butter in pieces and rub into the flour with the fingertips until the mixture resembles fine breadcrumbs. Stir in the sugar and 4 tablespoons of the lemon squash. Beat the eggs and add with the syrup. Mix well. Turn the mixture into the prepared tin and smooth the top. Cook in a moderate oven (180°C, 350°F, Gas Mark 4) for about 1 hour 10 minutes. Turn out and cool on a wire rack.

Make a small heart shape out of cardboard. Roll out the marzipan and use the heart shape as a guide to cut out marzipan hearts. Use these to decorate the cake.

To make your own marzipan, mix 25 g/1 oz ground almonds with 25 g/1 oz castor sugar and 50 g/2 oz icing sugar. Add beaten egg yolk to bind and almond essence to taste.

Store the cake in an airtight tin for 4–5 days.

Ginger and Date Ring

Approximate preparation time: 15 minutes
Cooking time: 55 minutes

75 g/3 oz dates
225 g/8 oz plain flour
pinch of salt
2 teaspoons ground ginger
1 teaspoon bicarbonate of soda
100 g/4 oz soft brown sugar
100 g/4 oz butter
75 g/3 oz treacle
75 g/3 oz golden syrup
1 egg
75 g/3 oz icing sugar

Grease a 20-cm/8-inch ring mould with butter.

Finely chop the dates. Sift the flour, salt, ginger and bicarbonate of soda into a bowl. Stir in the dates and make a well in the centre of the mixture.

Put the sugar, butter, treacle and syrup in a saucepan and heat gently until the sugar has dissolved. Do not boil. Cool then pour into the flour mixture. Beat the egg, add to the flour and mix all together. Turn into the prepared mould and bake in a moderate oven (160°C, 325°F, Gas Mark 3) for 55 minutes. Turn out and cool on a wire rack. The cake will sink slightly on cooling.

Sift the icing sugar and mix with enough water to make a soft icing. Pour this over the cake, allowing it to run down the sides.

Store the cake in an airtight tin for up to 5 days.

Chocolate and Treacle Cake

Approximate preparation time: 15 minutes
Cooking time: 1 hour 20 minutes

$1\frac{1}{2}$ tablespoons cocoa powder
50 g/2 oz margarine
50 g/2 oz granulated sugar
1 large egg
175 g/6 oz plain flour
$\frac{1}{2}$ teaspoon bicarbonate of soda
$2\frac{1}{2}$ tablespoons treacle
6 tablespoons warm milk
glacé cherries (optional)

Grease a deep 15-cm/6-inch round cake tin and line the base and sides with greaseproof paper.

Mix the cocoa with 3 tablespoons hot water and set aside to cool completely.

Cream the margarine with the sugar until light and fluffy. Beat the egg and add gradually to the creamed mixture with the cocoa.

Sift the flour with the bicarbonate of soda and mix the treacle with the warm milk. Fold the flour and treacle into the mixture alternately. Turn the mixture into the prepared tin and cook in a moderate oven (180°C, 350°F, Gas Mark 4) for about 1 hour 20 minutes. Cool in the tin. If liked, decorate the top with glacé cherry halves.

Store in an airtight tin for up to 3 days. If preferred, wrap closely in greaseproof paper and foil.

Coffee Party Cake

Approximate preparation time: 45 minutes
Cooking time: 30–40 minutes plus rising time

275–300 g/10–11 oz plain flour
$\frac{1}{2}$ teaspoon salt
50 g/2 oz margarine
15 g/$\frac{1}{2}$ oz castor sugar
15 g/$\frac{1}{2}$ oz fresh yeast
125 ml/$\frac{1}{4}$ pint lukewarm milk
1 egg
225 g/8 oz strawberry jam
25 g/1 oz sponge cake crumbs
2 tablespoons granulated sugar

Grease and flour a 1-kg/2-lb loaf tin.

Sift the flour and salt into a bowl and rub in the margarine until the mixture resembles fine breadcrumbs. Stir in the sugar. Make a well in the centre of the flour. Cream the yeast with the milk and beat in the egg. Add to the flour and mix to make a soft dough. Knead on a lightly floured surface for 2 minutes, or until smooth. Place in a large polythene bag and leave in a warm place until doubled in size, about 1 hour.

Turn the dough on to a lightly floured surface and roll to a 20 × 40-cm/8 × 16-inch oblong.

Mix the jam and crumbs together and spread to within 1 cm/$\frac{1}{2}$ inch of the edges of the dough. Roll up from the short side. Place in the prepared tin and leave for about 25 minutes, or until the dough reaches beyond the top of the tin. Bake in a moderately hot oven (200°C, 400°F, Gas Mark 6) for 30–40 minutes. It is cooked when the base sounds hollow when tapped.

Put the sugar in a saucepan and dissolve in 2 tablespoons water. Bring to the boil and cook for 2 minutes or until slightly syrupy Brush over the top of the cake.

Eat the same day.

Walnut Spice Cake

Approximate preparation time: 20 minutes
Cooking time: 30–35 minutes

175 g/6 oz self-raising flour
1 teaspoon baking powder
pinch of salt
$\frac{1}{4}$ teaspoon ground cinnamon
$\frac{1}{4}$ teaspoon ground mixed spice
25 g/1 oz walnut halves
175 g/6 oz soft margarine
3 large eggs
75 g/3 oz castor sugar
75 g/3 oz soft brown sugar
175 g/6 oz icing sugar
75 g/3 oz unsalted butter

Lightly grease and line the bases of two 19-cm/7$\frac{1}{2}$-inch sandwich tins.

Sift the flour, baking powder, salt, cinnamon and spice into a bowl.

Reserve a few walnut halves and chop the rest finely. Add the nuts to the flour then add the margarine, eggs and castor and brown sugars. Stir in 1 tablespoon warm water and beat well for about 2 minutes, using a wooden spoon. Divide the mixture between the tins. Smooth the tops and cook in a moderate oven (160°C, 325°F, Gas Mark 3) for 30–35 minutes.

Sift the icing sugar into a bowl and beat with the butter and a little water. Fit a piping bag with a medium star nozzle and fill the bag with the buttercream. Spread the remaining buttercream over the top of one of the cakes and sandwich the cakes together. Pipe swirls in a ring around the cake and press a piece of walnut on top of each one.

This cake can be frozen for up to 2 months. Thaw for 4–5 hours.

Coffee and Almond Cake

Approximate preparation time: 20 minutes
Cooking time: 55 minutes

175 g/6 oz margarine
175 g/6 oz castor sugar
3 eggs
few drops almond essence
175 g/6 oz self-raising flour
3 teaspoons instant coffee powder
4 teaspoons hot water
few cubes of sugar

Grease a deep 15-cm/6-inch round cake tin and line the base and sides with greaseproof paper.

Cream the margarine with the sugar until light and fluffy. Beat the eggs and add gradually to the creamed mixture, beating well. Divide the mixture in half and add a few drops of almond essence to one half. Sift half of the flour over the top and fold in with a metal spoon.

Dissolve the coffee in the hot water and beat into the second half of the mixture. Sift the remaining flour over the top and fold in. Spoon the two mixtures alternately into the prepared tin. Smooth the top and cook in a moderate oven (180°C, 350°F, Gas Mark 4) for 55 minutes or until cooked through.

Turn out and cool on a wire rack. Crush the sugar and sprinkle over the top of the cake.

This cake can be frozen. Store for up to 2 months. Thaw for 4–5 hours.

Walnut Spice Cake

Moist Coffee Ring

Approximate preparation time: 30 minutes
Cooking time: 50–55 minutes

100 g/4 oz butter
100 g/4 oz brown sugar
2 large eggs
2 tablespoons instant coffee powder
150 g/5 oz self-raising flour
100 g/4 oz granulated sugar
4 drops rum essence
150 ml/$\frac{1}{4}$ pint double cream
2 teaspoons icing sugar
few walnut halves

Grease a 20-cm/8-inch ring tin and dust with flour, shaking off any excess.

Cream the butter with the sugar until light and fluffy. Beat the eggs and add gradually to the creamed mixture. Dissolve the coffee in 3 tablespoons hot water. Allow to cool then add 1 tablespoon to the creamed mixture. Sift the flour over the top and fold in with a metal spoon. Turn into the prepared tin and cook in a moderate oven (180°C, 350°F, Gas Mark 4) for 40–45 minutes. Turn out and cool on a wire rack. Prick the top with a skewer. Put the sugar in a saucepan with 150 ml/$\frac{1}{4}$ pint water. Heat gently until the sugar dissolves. Boil for 2 minutes without colouring. Stir in the remaining coffee and the rum essence. Place the cake on a serving plate and spoon the syrup over the top.

Whip the cream with the icing sugar. Fit a piping bag with a medium star nozzle and fill the bag with the cream. Pipe around the top of the ring and decorate with walnuts.

Variation
Lemon Iced Ring Prepare as above, but omit the cream and nuts. Mix 50 g/2 oz icing sugar with lemon juice to make a coating icing. Spoon over the ring allowing it to run over the sides.

Either cake can be frozen, the latter without the icing. Store for up to 2 months. Thaw for 4–5 hours. Eat on the day of thawing.

Iced Cherry Ring

Approximate preparation time: 20 minutes plus rising time
Cooking time: 20 minutes

350 g/12 oz plain flour
pinch of salt
2 teaspoons castor sugar
50 g/2 oz butter
15 g/$\frac{1}{2}$ oz fresh yeast
5 tablespoons lukewarm milk
1 small egg
150 g/5 oz icing sugar
6 glacé cherries

Lightly flour a baking tray.

Sift the flour with the salt. Stir in the sugar and rub in the butter until the mixture resembles fine breadcrumbs. Cream the yeast with the 5 tablespoons lukewarm milk. Stir into the flour, add the egg and beat well. Knead for 10 minutes. Place the dough in a warm place for 45 minutes or until doubled in size.

Knead the dough for 2 minutes and divide into six rounds. Place these, just touching, in a ring on the baking tray. Cover and leave in a warm place for 15 minutes. Cook in a hot oven (220°C, 425°F, Gas Mark 7) for 20 minutes, or until golden. Leave to cool.

Sift the icing sugar and add enough water to make a coating icing. Spoon over the ring and decorate with the cherries.

Eat the same day or freeze, without the icing and cherries for up to 2 months. Thaw for 4–5 hours.

Variation
Sunday Teatime Ring Make just as above, but omit the cherries. Split the ring through the middle and sandwich together with whipped cream.

Eat the same day, or freeze without the cream for up to 2 months. Thaw for 4–5 hours.

GATEAUX

Apricot Choux Ring

Approximate preparation time: 20
minutes
Cooking time: 1 hour

65 g/$2\frac{1}{2}$ oz plain flour
50 g/2 oz margarine
2 large eggs
100 g/4 oz icing sugar
15 g/$\frac{1}{2}$ oz cocoa powder
little unsweetened black coffee
150 ml/$\frac{1}{4}$ pint double cream
2 tablespoons milk
1 (425-g/15-oz) can apricot halves

Line a large baking tray with foil and mark
out a 15-cm/6-inch ring on it.

Sift the flour. Put the margarine in a
saucepan with 150 ml/$\frac{1}{4}$ pint water. Heat to
melt the margarine, then bring to the boil.
Add the flour and cook, stirring for 2 minutes. The mixture should come away
cleanly from the sides of the pan. Remove
from the heat. Beat the eggs and add
gradually to the flour mixture, beating
thoroughly.

Fit a piping bag with a 1-cm/$\frac{1}{2}$-inch plain
nozzle and fill the bag with the mixture. Pipe
balls of the mixture around the ring on the
baking tray. Cook in a hot oven (220°C,
425°F, Gas Mark 7) for about 40 minutes
until crisp and golden. Leave to cool.

Sift the icing sugar and cocoa together
and add enough black coffee to make a
coating icing.

Split the ring through the middle. Whip
the cream and milk together and use to
sandwich the halves together. Spoon the
icing over the top. Drain the apricots and put
the fruit in the centre.

Eat the same day.

Meringue Layer

Approximate preparation time: 25
minutes
Cooking time: 3 hours

4 egg whites
225 g/8 oz castor sugar
100 g/4 oz icing sugar
50 g/2 oz unsalted butter
strong, unsweetened black coffee
to taste
150 ml/$\frac{1}{4}$ pint double cream
8–12 raspberries
15 g/$\frac{1}{2}$ oz chopped almonds
canned peach halves

Line a large baking tray with foil or bakewell
paper. Mark out two 20-cm/8-inch rounds.

Whisk the egg whites until very stiff and
standing in peaks. Whisk in half the sugar, a
teaspoon at a time. Whisk until stiff and
glossy, then fold in the remaining sugar.
Spoon the mixture over the circles on the
baking tray and cook in a cool oven (140°C,
275°F, Gas Mark 1) for 3 hours, or until
completely dry. Sift the icing sugar and beat
with the butter until light and creamy. Add
cold black coffee to taste. Use this butter
cream to sandwich the two meringues
together.

Whip the cream and use to decorate the
cake with the raspberries, almonds and
peach halves.

Eat the same day, or store the meringues,
unfilled, in an airtight tin for up to 3 days.

Meringue Raspberry Sandwich

Approximate preparation time: 25 minutes
Cooking time: $2\frac{3}{4}$ hours

1 large egg, separated
65 g/$2\frac{1}{2}$ oz castor sugar
100 g/4 oz self-raising flour
50 g/2 oz butter
few drops almond essence
175 g/6 oz fresh or thawed frozen raspberries
25 g/1 oz icing sugar

Line a baking tray with foil and mark a 15-cm/6-inch round on it.

Whisk the egg white until very stiff and standing in peaks. Gradually whisk in 50 g/2 oz of the castor sugar. Spread half the mixture over the marked round on the baking tray. Fit a piping bag with a medium star nozzle and fill the bag with the remaining meringue. Pipe 13 swirls around the top edge then cook in a very cool oven (110°C, 225°F, Gas Mark $\frac{1}{4}$) for $2\frac{1}{2}$ hours. Reduce the heat if the meringue starts to brown.

Sift the flour and add the remaining sugar. Rub in the butter until the mixture resembles fine breadcrumbs. Add the egg yolk, almond essence and enough water to make a stiff dough. Roll out to an 18-cm/7-inch round and place on a greased baking tray. Prick all over and bake in a moderately hot oven (190°C, 375°F, Gas Mark 5) for 15 minutes.

Reserve 13 raspberries for the top. Place the rest on the pastry. Sift the icing sugar on top, cover with the meringue and place a raspberry on each piped swirl.

Cream Layer

Approximate preparation time: 30 minutes
Cooking time: 1 hour 10 minutes

175 g/6 oz castor sugar
175 g/6 oz margarine
3 large eggs
225 g/8 oz self-raising flour
grated rind of 1 small lemon
450 ml/$\frac{3}{4}$ pint double cream
1 tablespoon lemon curd
1 tablespoon red jam

Grease an 18-cm/7-inch round cake tin. Line with greased greaseproof paper.

Cream the sugar and margarine until light and fluffy. Beat the eggs and add gradually to the creamed mixture, beating alternately with spoonfuls of sifted flour. Sift the rest of the flour over the top and fold in with the lemon rind, using a metal spoon. Turn into the prepared tin and cook in a moderate oven (180°C, 350°F, Gas Mark 4) for about 1 hour 10 minutes. Cool on a wire rack and slice through into three layers.

Whip the cream and use some to sandwich the layers together. Spread cream over the top. Fit a piping bag with a small star nozzle and fill the bag with the remaining cream. Pipe nine rings around the top of the cake and fill some with lemon curd, some with jam.

Eat the same day or freeze for up to 2 months. Thaw for 4–5 hours.

Tub of Grapes

Approximate preparation time: 25
minutes
Cooking time: 45–50 minutes

100 g/4 oz self-raising flour
$\frac{1}{2}$ teaspoon baking powder
225 g/8 oz soft margarine
100 g/4 oz castor sugar
2 large eggs
100 g/4 oz black and green grapes
250 g/9 oz icing sugar
1 tablespoon rum, or few drops
rum essence
1 (112-g/4-oz) packet sponge
fingers

Grease an 18-cm/7-inch round cake tin and line the base with greaseproof paper.

Sift the flour and baking powder into a bowl. Add half the margarine, the sugar and eggs and beat with a wooden spoon for 2–3 minutes until smooth. Turn into the prepared tin and cook in a moderate oven (180°C, 350°F, Gas Mark 4) for 45–50 minutes. Turn out and cool on a wire rack.

Halve the grapes and remove the pips. Sift the icing sugar and beat with the remaining margarine and rum or essence until creamy. Split the cake through the middle and sandwich together with half the buttercream and half the grapes. Spread a little buttercream on the sides of the cake. Cut the sponge fingers in half and press them on to the sides of the cake. Arrange the remaining grapes on top. Fit a piping bag with a medium star nozzle and fill the bag with the cream. Pipe a decoration on top.

Eat the same day.

Banana Surprise

Approximate preparation time: 25
minutes
Cooking time: 50 minutes

175 g/6 oz margarine
175 g/6 oz soft brown sugar
3 large eggs
175 g/6 oz self-raising flour
2 teaspoons baking powder
2 small bananas
150 ml/$\frac{1}{4}$ pint plus 2 tablespoons
double cream
4 tablespoons cold water
50 g/2 oz granulated sugar
2 teaspoons instant coffee powder
1 tablespoon rum
1 tablespoon lemon juice

Grease a 1-kg/2-lb loaf tin and line the base and sides with greased foil.

Put the margarine in a bowl with the sugar, eggs, flour and baking powder and beat with a wooden spoon for about 3 minutes or until smooth. Turn into the prepared tin, smooth the top and cook in a moderately hot oven (190°C, 375°F, Gas Mark 5) for about 50 minutes. Turn out and cool upside down on a wire rack.

Turn over and mark an oblong 5 × 15 cm/ 2 × 6 inches on top of the cake. Scoop out 3 tablespoons of the cake and reduce this to crumbs. Slice one banana and mix with the crumbs. Whip the cream and add 2 tablespoons to the banana mixture. Press this back into the cake. Turn the cake upside down and prick well with a fork. Heat the water and sugar gently until all the granules have dissolved. Bring to the boil and boil for 3 minutes. Dissolve the coffee in 2 tablespoons hot water and add to the syrup with the rum. Spoon this over the cake. Fit a piping bag with a medium star nozzle and fill the bag with the remaining cream. Pipe rosettes on the top of the cake. Slice the remaining banana, toss in the lemon juice and use for decoration.

Freeze without the banana topping for up to 2 months. Thaw for 4–5 hours.

Yogurt Cake

Approximate preparation time: 20
minutes
Cooking time: 25 minutes

50 g/2 oz castor sugar
50 g/2 oz soft brown sugar
100 g/4 oz margarine
2 eggs
150 g/5 oz self-raising flour
1 (142-ml/5-fl oz) carton raspberry
yogurt
few fresh raspberries or thawed
frozen ones

Lightly grease the bases of two 16.5-cm/6$\frac{1}{2}$-inch sandwich tins and line with grease-proof paper.

Cream both sugars with the margarine until light and fluffy.

Beat the eggs and add gradually to the creamed mixture. Sift the flour over the top and fold in using a metal spoon. Turn into the prepared tins and cook in a moderately hot oven (190°C, 375°F, Gas Mark 5) for about 25 minutes. Turn out and cool on a wire rack.

Sandwich the cakes together with half the yogurt and spread the rest on top. Decorate with the raspberries.

Variations
Pineapple Yogurt Cake Make just as for the Raspberry Yogurt Cake using pineapple yogurt. Omit the raspberries and use melted chocolate cake covering to make curls. Sprinkle over the cake. Plain chocolate can be used, but it will discolour in 4–5 hours.

Strawberry Gâteau

Approximate preparation time: 25
minutes
Cooking time: 25 minutes

50 g/2 oz butter
50 g/2 oz castor sugar
1 large egg
50 g/2 oz self-raising flour
300 ml/$\frac{1}{2}$ pint double cream
225 g/8 oz firm strawberries
2–3 tablespoons strawberry jam
1–2 tablespoons brandy

Lightly grease a 19-cm/7$\frac{1}{2}$-inch sandwich tin and line the base with greaseproof paper.

Cream the butter with the sugar until light and fluffy. Beat the egg and add gradually to the creamed mixture.

Sift the flour over the top and fold in with a metal spoon. Turn the mixture into the prepared tin and smooth the top. Cook in a moderately hot oven (190°C, 375°F, Gas Mark 5) for 25 minutes or until firm. Turn out and cool on a wire rack.

Whip the cream and pile it on top of the cold cake. Hull the strawberries and arrange on the cream.

Heat the jam with 1 tablespoon water and the brandy, allow to cool then pour over the strawberries.

Eat the same day. The cake base may be frozen and stored for up to 2 months. Thaw for 4–5 hours.

Three-tier Gâteau

Approximate preparation time: 40 minutes
Cooking time: 1 hour 10 minutes

150 g/6 oz castor sugar
175 g/6 oz butter
3 large eggs
200 g/7 oz self-raising flour
1 tablespoon milk
1 teaspoon finely grated lemon rind
450 ml/$\frac{3}{4}$ pint double cream
2 large peaches
2 tablespoons strained orange juice

Grease a deep 18-cm/7-inch cake tin and line the base and sides with greaseproof paper.

Cream the sugar and butter together until light and fluffy. Beat the eggs and add gradually to the creamed mixture, beating well.

Sift the flour over the top and fold in with a metal spoon. Add enough milk to make a soft dropping consistency. Stir in the lemon rind. Turn the mixture into the prepared tin and smooth the top. Cook in a moderate oven (180°C, 350°F, Gas Mark 4) for about 1 hour 10 minutes, or until firm to the touch.

Turn out and cool on a wire rack. When completely cold, use a sharp knife to cut the cake into three layers.

Whip the cream until thick and peel the peaches. This is easier if you blanch them in boiling water for 30 seconds. Halve the peaches and remove the stones. Cut the flesh into fairly thick slices and toss in the orange juice to prevent discoloration. Sandwich the cake together with the cream and peach slices. Once filled, eat within 2 hours.

The unfilled cake can be frozen and stored for up to 2 months. Thaw for 4–5 hours.

Variations

Use any other fresh fruit in season and if liked add one of the following toppings.
Filling One: Heat a little peach or apricot jam and brush all over the top of the gâteau.
Filling Two: Heat 100 g/4 oz sugar with 3 tablespoons water until dissolved then boil until caramel-coloured. Pour on to a lightly oiled baking tray and leave until cold and hard. Break up with a rolling pin and use with whipped cream to decorate the top of the cake.
Topping Three: Place a large paper doily on top of the cake. Sift icing sugar over the top and then remove the doily carefully, leaving the pattern of the doily on the cake.

Party Hazelnut Ring

Approximate preparation time: 30 minutes
Cooking time: 50–55 minutes

100 g/4 oz butter
100 g/4 oz soft brown sugar
2 large eggs
2 tablespoons instant coffee powder
3 tablespoons brandy
150 g/5 oz self-raising flour
100 g/4 oz granulated sugar
150 ml/$\frac{1}{4}$ pint double cream
2 teaspoons icing sugar
skinned hazelnuts for decoration

Make exactly as for Moist coffee ring, (see page 56) but use the 3 tablespoons brandy and the water to dissolve the coffee powder.

Omit the rum essence and use hazelnuts instead of walnuts for decoration.

You can freeze this cake. Pack in a plastic box leaving plenty of room at the top. Cover with a tightly fitting lid.

If liked, some grated plain chocolate can be sprinkled over the top of the cake when it has thawed completely.

Three-tier Gâteau

Strawberry Star

Approximate preparation time: 30 minutes
Cooking time: 20–25 minutes

175 g/6 oz margarine
175 g/6 oz castor sugar
3 large eggs
few drops vanilla essence
115 g/4$\frac{1}{2}$ oz plain flour
40 g/1$\frac{1}{2}$ oz cornflour
$\frac{1}{2}$ teaspoon baking powder
300 ml/$\frac{1}{2}$ pint double cream
2$\frac{1}{2}$ tablespoons strawberry jam

Grease two 20-cm/8-inch sandwich tins and line the bases with greaseproof paper.

Cream the margarine and sugar together until light and fluffy. Beat the eggs and add gradually to the creamed mixture. Beat in the vanilla essence. Sift the flour, cornflour and baking powder over the top and fold in with a metal spoon. Divide between the prepared tins, smooth the tops and cook in a moderately hot oven (190°C, 375°F, Gas Mark 5) for 20–25 minutes or until firm. Turn out and cool on a wire rack.

Whip the cream until thick. Cut out a large star shape from the centre of one cake. Spread two-thirds of the cream over the whole cake and spread with the jam. Place the other cake on top. Fit a piping bag with a small star nozzle and fill the bag with the cream. Pipe a design around the edges of the top cake.

The undecorated cake can be frozen and stored for up to 2 months. Thaw for 4–5 hours.

Lemon and Orange Gâteau

Approximate preparation time: 25 minutes
Cooking time: 25 minutes

175 g/6 oz margarine
175 g/6 oz castor sugar
3 large eggs
3 tablespoons lemon curd
175 g/6 oz self-raising flour
300 ml/$\frac{1}{2}$ pint double cream
5 tablespoons orange curd

Lightly grease two 20-cm/8-inch sandwich tins and line the bases with greaseproof paper.

Cream the margarine and sugar together until light and fluffy. Beat the eggs and add gradually to the creamed mixture. Beat in 1 tablespoon of the lemon curd. Sift the flour over the top and fold in with a metal spoon. Divide the mixture between the prepared tins and cook in a moderately hot oven (200°C, 400°F, Gas Mark 6) for 25 minutes. Turn out and cool on a wire rack.

Whip the cream and spread half of it on one cake. Spread over 3 tablespoons of the orange curd. Place the other cake on top. Spread half the remaining cream over the top. Fit a piping bag with a small star nozzle and fill the bag with the remaining cream. Pipe lines to divide the cake in eight slices and fill the segments with orange and lemon curd alternately.

Eat the same day or freeze and store for up to 2 months. Thaw for 4–5 hours.

Marmalade and Ginger Cake

Approximate preparation time: 20 minutes
Cooking time: 15 minutes

175 g/6 oz unsalted butter
90 g/3½ oz soft brown sugar
2 large eggs
2 tablespoons orange jelly marmalade, sieved
100 g/4 oz self-raising flour
1½ teaspoons ground ginger
175 g/6 oz icing sugar
1 tablespoon orange squash

Grease a 24×33-cm/9½×13½-inch Swiss roll tin and line with greaseproof paper.

Cream 100 g/4 oz of the butter with the sugar until light and fluffy. Beat the eggs and add gradually to the creamed mixture. Beat in 1 tablespoon of the marmalade. Sift the flour and ginger over the top and fold in with a metal spoon. Spread over the prepared tin and cook in a moderate oven (180°C, 350°F, Gas Mark 4) for about 15 minutes. Cool on a wire rack.

Sift the icing sugar and beat in the remaining butter until smooth. Beat in the orange squash. Cut the cake into three and sandwich together with two-thirds of the buttercream. Spread the remaining marmalade on top. Fit a piping bag with a small star nozzle and fill the bag with the remaining buttercream. Pipe a pattern on top of the cake.

Eat the same day or freeze and store for up to 2 months. Thaw for 4–5 hours.

Almond Layer Cake

Approximate preparation time: 30 minutes
Cooking time: 20 minutes

275 g/10 oz butter
175 g/6 oz castor sugar
3 eggs
few drops almond essence
175 g/6 oz self-raising flour
225 g/8 oz icing sugar
1 tablespoon brandy
glacé cherries and angelica (optional)

Lightly grease a 30×35-cm/12×14-inch meat tin and line the base with greaseproof paper.

Cream 175 g/6 oz of the butter with the sugar until light and fluffy. Beat the eggs and add gradually to the creamed mixture. Beat in the almond essence. Sift the flour over the top and fold in with a metal spoon. Turn the mixture into the prepared tin and cook in a moderately hot oven (190°C, 375°F, Gas Mark 5) for 20 minutes or until firm. Leave to cool.

Sift the icing sugar and beat with the remaining butter and the brandy and almond essence to taste. Trim the edges of the cake and cut in quarters. Sandwich the pieces together with buttercream and spread the rest of the buttercream on top. Mark a pattern in the cream using a knife edge. Decorate with cherries and angelica if liked.

This cake can be frozen. Store for up to 2 months. Thaw for 4–5 hours.

Hazelnut Roll

Approximate preparation time: 40
minutes
Cooking time: 10–12 minutes

1 teaspoon grated orange rind
4 large eggs
115 g/4½ oz castor sugar
100 g/4 oz self-raising flour
300 ml/½ pint double cream
40 g/1½ oz hazelnuts, very finely
chopped
grated chocolate (optional)

Grease a 23×33-cm/9×13-inch Swiss roll tin. Line with greased greaseproof paper.

Put the orange rind, eggs and sugar in a bowl. Stand the bowl over a pan of hot water (not over heat) and whisk until thick. The whisk should leave a trail visible for 5 seconds. Remove the bowl from the pan. Sift the flour over the top and fold in with a metal spoon. Spread over the prepared tin and cook in a hot oven (220°C, 475°F, Gas Mark 7) for 10–12 minutes.

Sprinkle a little castor sugar on a piece of greaseproof paper and turn the cake out on to it. Remove the greased paper. Trim the edges then roll up around the paper. Unroll the cake. Whip the cream and spread two-thirds on the cake. Roll up again. Spread more cream over the sides and ends and cover with nuts. Pipe the remaining cream over the top. If liked, sprinkle with grated chocolate.

Iced Mocha Cake

Approximate preparation time: 30
minutes
Cooking time: 35 minutes

100 g/4 oz margarine
100 g/4 oz soft brown sugar
2 large eggs
3 teaspoons instant coffee powder
100 g/4 oz self-raising flour
3 tablespoons chocolate spread
225 g/8 oz icing sugar

Grease a 19-cm/7½-inch sandwich tin and line the base with greaseproof paper.

Cream the margarine and sugar until light and fluffy. Beat the eggs and add gradually to the creamed mixture. Dissolve the coffee in 1 tablespoon boiling water, leave to cool and add to the creamed mixture. Sift the flour over the top and fold in with a metal spoon. Turn the mixture into the prepared tin and cook in a moderate oven (180°C, 350°F, Gas Mark 4) for 35 minutes. Turn out and cool on a wire rack.

Split the cake through the middle and sandwich together with 2 tablespoons of the chocolate spread. Fit a piping bag with a fine plain nozzle and fill the bag with the spread.

Sift the icing sugar and mix with water to make a coating icing. Pour over the cake and immediately pipe four concentric circles of chocolate spread on the cake. Take a skewer and draw it from the centre of the cake to the edge. Wipe and repeat three more times to divide the cake in quarters. Draw the skewer from the outside to the centre to divide the cake in eight and make a spider's web effect.

Freeze the undecorated cake for up to 2 months. Thaw for 4–5 hours.

Coffee and Raisin Cake

Approximate preparation time: 30 minutes
Cooking time: 50 minutes

100 g/4 oz margarine
75 g/3 oz castor sugar
50 g/2 oz golden syrup
2 large eggs
1½ tablespoons coffee essence
50 g/2 oz seedless raisins, chopped
100 g/4 oz self-raising flour
150 ml/¼ pint double cream
225 g/8 oz icing sugar
40 g/1½ oz flaked almonds, toasted

Grease a 20-cm/8-inch round cake tin and line the base and sides with greaseproof paper.

Cream the margarine with the sugar until light and fluffy. Beat the syrup, eggs and ½ tablespoon of the coffee essence together and gradually beat into the creamed mixture. Mix in the raisins. Sift the flour over the top and fold in with a metal spoon. Turn into the prepared tin, smooth the top and cook in a moderate oven (180°C, 350°F, Gas Mark 4) for about 50 minutes. Turn out and cool on a wire rack.

Whip the cream until thick. Split the cake through the middle and sandwich together with two-thirds of the cream. Sift the icing sugar and mix with 3 tablespoons boiling water. Fit a piping bag with a fine plain nozzle and put 2 tablespoons of the icing in the bag. Mix the remaining coffee essence with the spare icing.

Spread the remaining cream around the sides of the cake and press on the almonds. Pour the coffee icing over the top and quickly pipe parallel lines of white icing across it. Quickly run a skewer at right angles across the piped lines to give a feather effect.

The undecorated cake can be frozen and stored for up to 2 months. Thaw for 4–5 hours.

Coffee Square

Approximate preparation time: 30 minutes
Cooking time: 35 minutes

225 g/8 oz unsalted butter
100 g/4 oz castor sugar
50 g/2 oz soft brown sugar
3 large eggs
15 g/½ oz desiccated coconut
1 tablespoon orange squash
1½ tablespoons instant coffee powder
½ teaspoon ground cinnamon
175 g/6 oz self-raising flour
350 g/12 oz icing sugar
whisky to taste
25 g/1 oz flaked almonds (optional)
crystallised orange and lemon slices for decoration

Grease a deep 20-cm/8-inch square cake tin. Line the base with greaseproof paper.

Cream 175 g/6 oz of the butter and the two sugars together until light and fluffy. Beat the eggs and add gradually to the creamed mixture. Stir in the coconut and orange squash. Sift 2 teaspoons of the coffee with the cinnamon and flour over the top and fold in with a metal spoon. Turn the mixture into the prepared tin and cook in a moderately hot oven (200°C, 400°F, Gas Mark 6) for about 35 minutes. Turn out and cool on a wire rack.

Put the remaining butter and coffee powder in a saucepan with 3 tablespoons water. Heat gently to melt the butter. Sift the icing sugar and beat in the butter mixture and whisky. Fit a piping bag with a small star nozzle and put 2 tablespoons of the icing in the bag. Spread the remaining icing over the cake and rough up with a knife. Pipe a decoration on top and add the almonds (if used) orange and lemon slices.

This cake can be frozen. Store for up to 2 months. Thaw for 4–5 hours.

Chocolate Cream Cake

Approximate preparation time: 20 minutes
Cooking time: 50–55 minutes

100 g/4 oz plain chocolate
200 g/7 oz soft brown sugar
2 tablespoons milk
few drops vanilla essence
150 g/5 oz margarine
3 large eggs
225 g/8 oz self-raising flour
1 tablespoon rum
225 g/8 oz apricot jam
300 ml/½ pint double cream
hazelnuts (optional)

Grease a 20-cm/8-inch cake tin and line the base and sides with greaseproof paper.

Break up the chocolate and put in a saucepan with 75 g/3 oz of the sugar, the milk and vanilla essence. Stir over a low heat until melted. Leave to cool but not harden.

Cream the margarine with the remaining sugar until light and fluffy. Beat the eggs and add gradually to the creamed mixture. Sift the flour over the top and fold in with the chocolate mixture. Turn into the prepared tin, smooth the top and cook in a moderately hot oven (190°C, 375°F, Gas Mark 5) for 40–45 minutes. Turn out and cool on a wire rack.

Mix the rum and jam together. Whip the cream until stiff. Split the cake into three layers. Sandwich back together with two-thirds of the jam and cream. Spread the remaining jam on top. Fit a piping bag with a small star nozzle and fill the bag with the remaining cream. Pipe a design around the top and decorate with the hazelnuts if liked.

This cake can be frozen. Store for up to 2 months. Thaw for 4–5 hours.

Chocolate Gâteau

Approximate preparation time: 35 minutes
Cooking time: 25 minutes

175 g/6 oz castor sugar
250 g/9 oz margarine
3 large eggs
150 g/5 oz self-raising flour
75 g/3 oz cocoa powder
575 g/1 lb 4 oz icing sugar
2 tablespoons milk
rum to taste
2 teaspoons powdered gelatine
20 g/¾ oz soft white fat (not lard)

Grease two 19-cm/7½-inch sandwich tins and line the bases with greaseproof paper.

Cream the sugar and 175 g/6 oz of the margarine together until light and fluffy. Beat the eggs and add gradually to the creamed mixture. Sift the flour and 25 g/1 oz of the cocoa over the top and fold in with a metal spoon. Turn into the prepared tins and cook in a moderately hot oven (190°C, 375°F, Gas Mark 5) for about 25 minutes. Turn out and cool on a wire rack.

Sift 150 g/5 oz of the icing sugar with 25 g/1 oz of the cocoa. Beat in the remaining margarine with the milk and rum. Split both cakes in two through the middle and sandwich the layers together with the buttercream.

Dissolve the gelatine in 4 tablespoons water in a small bowl over a pan of hot water. When dissolved, beat in the fat. Remove from the heat. Sift the remaining icing sugar and cocoa together and mix in the gelatine mixture. Knead until smooth.

Roll out two-thirds of the icing and use to cover the cake. Divide the rest into four and roll each piece to a 10-cm/4-inch round. Stretch the edges lightly to make shapes and use to decorate the cake.

Eat within 2 days. The un-iced cake can be frozen. Store for up to 2 months. Thaw for 4–5 hours.

PASTRIES AND PIES

Jam Slice

Approximate preparation time: 15 minutes
Cooking time: 30 minutes

25 g/1 oz glacé cherries
5 tablespoons apricot jam
50 g/2 oz chopped mixed peel
1 (370-g/13-oz) packet frozen puff pastry, thawed
1 egg
little extra flour

Chop the cherries and mix with the jam and peel.

Roll out the pastry on a lightly floured surface to a 23-cm/9-inch square. Cut into two rectangles. Place one piece on a baking tray, spread the jam mixture on top, leaving a 1-cm/$\frac{1}{2}$-inch border.

Beat the egg and brush the edges of the pastry. Sprinkle a little flour on the second piece of pastry and fold in half lengthways. Make cuts about 5-cm/2-inches long about 1-cm/$\frac{1}{2}$-inch apart down the folded edge. Open out the pastry and place over the jam covered piece. Seal, flake and flute the edges and brush the top with beaten egg.

Cook in a hot oven (220°C, 425°F, Gas Mark 7) for about 30 minutes.

Eat the same day.

Fruit Puff

Approximate preparation time: 30 minutes
Cooking time: 20 minutes
Serves 4–5

1 (370-g/13-oz) packet frozen puff pastry thawed
1 small egg yolk
1 medium red-skinned dessert apple
juice of 1 small lemon
1 (227-g/8-oz) can red cherries
1 (227-g/8-oz) can peach slices
few canned apricot halves
100 g/4 oz black grapes
2 teaspoons honey or warmed apricot jam

Damp a baking tray.

Roll out the pastry on a lightly floured surface to a 15×25-cm/6×10-inch rectangle. Cut off a 1-cm/$\frac{1}{2}$-inch strip all the way round. Beat the egg yolk and brush the edges of the pastry. Place the strips on the edges to make a frame and mark with a knife in a criss-cross pattern. Brush the edges with egg yolk and place the pastry on the baking tray. Cook in a moderately hot oven (200°C, 400°F, Gas Mark 6) for about 20 minutes. Leave to cool.

Press the centre of the pastry down to make a hollow. Core and slice the apple and toss in the lemon juice. Drain the cherries, peaches and apricots. Arrange all the fruit in the pastry case and brush with the honey or apricot jam.

Eat the same day.

Pear and Ginger Jalousie

Approximate preparation time: 25 minutes
Cooking time: 20–25 minutes

1 (212-g/7½-oz) packet frozen puff pastry, thawed
1 egg
2 large pears
50 g/2 oz stem ginger

Damp a baking tray.

Roll out the pastry on a lightly floured surface to a 25×30-cm/10×12-inch rectangle. Cut the pastry in half through the long sides. Cut a 5-mm/¼-inch strip from all round the edge of one piece. Beat the egg and brush over the cut strip. Fit the strip back on the edge of the pastry to make a rectangular flan.

Peel, core and slice the pears and place in the flan. Chop the ginger and sprinkle over the pears.

Brush the rim of the pastry with egg. Fold the remaining pastry and slash it through the fold at 1-cm/½-inch intervals to within 1 cm/½ inch of the edges. Unfold and seal on to the base. Brush the whole with beaten egg and cook in a hot oven (220°C, 425°F, Gas Mark 7) for 20–25 minutes. Serve hot with a sweet sauce.

Eat the same day.

Banana Pastry Puff

Approximate preparation time: 40 minutes
Cooking time: 30 minutes

1 (212-g/7½-oz) packet frozen puff pastry, thawed
1 medium banana
225 g/8 oz cooking apples
grated rind and juice of ½ lemon
50 g/2 oz raisins
25 g/1 oz plain biscuits
1 tablespoon granulated sugar
1 small egg white

Damp a baking tray.

Roll out the pastry on a lightly floured surface. Cut out a 23-cm/9-inch round and a 20-cm/8-inch round. Place the smaller round on the baking tray and prick all over with a fork.

Mash the banana. Peel, core and chop the apples. Mix the banana and apple and add the lemon juice and rind and the raisins. Crush the biscuits finely and stir in with half the sugar. Spoon over the pastry on the baking tray. Lightly beat the egg white and brush over the pastry edges. Place the other round on top, pressing the edges to seal.

Brush the top with egg white and mark in a lattice pattern with a knife. Sprinkle with the remaining sugar and cook in a hot oven (220°C, 425°F, Gas Mark 7) for about 30 minutes.

Eat the same day.

Variation

If liked use drained canned prunes with the banana and biscuits for the filling.

Apple and Apricot Layer

Approximate preparation time: 25
minutes plus standing time
Cooking time: 25 minutes

350 g/12 oz flaky pastry mix
450 g/1 lb cooking apples
225 g/8 oz apricot jam
$\frac{1}{4}$ teaspoon ground cinnamon
300 ml/$\frac{1}{2}$ pint milk
1 tablespoon custard powder
2 tablespoons castor sugar
2 tablespoons fresh cream

Damp two baking trays.

Make up the pastry according to the instructions on the packet. Place in a polythene bag and chill for 10 minutes. Roll out on a lightly floured board and cut out three 18-cm/7-inch rounds. Collect the trimmings together and roll out another 18-cm/7-inch round. Place the rounds on the baking trays. Cook in a hot oven (220°C, 425°F, Gas Mark 7) for about 15 minutes.

Peel, core and roughly chop the apples. Place in a saucepan with the jam and cinnamon. Cook over a low heat for 10 minutes. Set aside to cool.

Use the custard powder and sugar to make custard, according to the instructions on the custard powder packet. Leave to cool. Whip the cream and stir into the custard. Sandwich the pastry layers together with the fruit mixture and custard. Eat the same day.

Fruit Lasagne Pie

Approximate preparation time: 20
minutes
Cooking time: 50 minutes
Serves 6–8

75 g/3 oz lasagne
1 (212-g/7$\frac{1}{2}$-oz) packet frozen puff
pastry, thawed
1 (425-g/15-oz) can peach slices
1 (425-g/15-oz) can custard
2 eggs
40 g/1$\frac{1}{2}$ oz walnuts, chopped
3 thin-skinned oranges
4 tablespoons marmalade

Cook the lasagne in boiling salted water until tender, about 12 minutes. Drain and put in a bowl of cold water.

Roll out the pastry on a lightly floured surface and use to line a 20-cm/8-inch flan dish. Prick the base with a fork.

Drain and chop the peaches and mix with the custard, eggs, 25 g/1 oz of the nuts and the finely grated rind of 1 orange. Layer the lasagne with this mixture, finishing with a peach layer.

Remove the rind and pith from the remaining oranges and cut the flesh in thin slices. Place on top of the flan. Cook in a moderately hot oven (190°C, 375°F, Gas Mark 5) for 40 minutes. Melt the marmalade and spoon over the top. Sprinkle with the remaining nuts.

Eat the same day.

Bakewell Pudding

Approximate preparation time: 20
minutes
Cooking time: 35–40 minutes
Serves 4

100 g/4 oz frozen puff pastry,
thawed
2 tablespoons raspberry jam
50 g/2 oz butter or margarine
50 g/2 oz castor sugar
grated rind and juice of $\frac{1}{2}$ small
lemon
1 egg
75 g/3 oz cake crumbs, sieved
75 g/3 oz ground almonds

Roll out the pastry on a lightly floured board and use to line a deep 18-cm/7-inch pie plate. Spread the jam over the base. Cream the butter or margarine and sugar with the lemon rind until light and fluffy. Beat the egg and add gradually to the creamed mixture. Mix the cake crumbs and ground almonds and fold into the mixture with the lemon juice to make a soft dropping consistency. Spread the mixture over the pastry case. Cook in a hot oven (220°C, 425°F, Gas Mark 7) for 15 minutes until turning brown. Reduce to moderate (180°C, 350°F, Gas Mark 4) and cook for a further 20–25 minutes.

This pie can be frozen. Store for up to 6 months.

Accompaniments
This is good with cream, ice cream or raspberry Melba sauce.

Apricot Cherry Pie

Approximate preparation time: 20
minutes
Cooking time: 35 minutes
Serves 4–5

225 g/8 oz plain flour
pinch of salt
50 g/2 oz margarine
50 g/2 oz lard
15 g/$\frac{1}{2}$ oz castor sugar
1 (312-g/11-oz) can cherries
1 (793-g/1 lb 12-oz) can apricots
1 egg

Sift the flour and salt into a bowl. Cut the margarine and lard into pieces and rub into the flour with the fingertips until the mixture resembles fine breadcrumbs. Stir in the sugar. Add cold water to make a firm dough. Roll out half the pastry on a lightly floured surface and use to line a 20-cm/8-inch pie plate. Drain the cherries and apricots, mix together and use to fill the pie plate. Damp the pastry edges with water. Roll out the remaining pastry and use as a lid for the pie. Seal, flake and flute the edges and use the trimmings to make decorations.

Beat the egg and brush the pie all over. Make a hole in the centre for the steam to escape. Place on a baking tray and cook in a moderately hot oven (200°C, 400°F, Gas Mark 6) for about 35 minutes.

This pie can be frozen. Store for up to 6 months.

Peach Pie

Approximate preparation time: 20
minutes
Cooking time: 35 minutes
Serves 4–5

225 g/8 oz plain flour
pinch of salt
50 g/2 oz margarine
50 g/2 oz lard
15 g/$\frac{1}{2}$ oz castor sugar
1 egg yolk
1 (793-g/1 lb 12-oz) can peach
halves
1 egg
castor sugar to sprinkle

Sift the flour and salt into a bowl. Cut the margarine and lard into pieces and rub into the flour with the fingertips until the mixture resembles fine breadcrumbs. Stir in the sugar and egg yolk with enough cold water to make a firm dough. Roll out half the pastry on a lightly floured surface and use to line a deep 20-cm/8-inch pie plate.

Drain the peaches and fill the pie plate with the fruit. Damp the edges of the pastry with water. Roll out the remaining pastry to make a lid. Seal flake and flute the edges. Roll out any trimmings and make into decorations. Beat the egg and use to glaze the pie. Leave a hole for steam to escape. Sprinkle with castor sugar and cook in a moderately hot oven (200°C, 400°F, Gas Mark 6) for about 35 minutes.

Serve hot or cold. The pie can be frozen for up to 4 months.

Accompaniments
The pie is delicious with raspberry ripple ice cream or a jam sauce.

Rhubarb and Orange Pie

Approximate preparation time: 20
minutes
Cooking time: 35 minutes
Serves 4–6

225 g/8 oz plain flour
pinch of salt
50 g/2 oz margarine
50 g/2 oz lard
15 g/$\frac{1}{2}$ oz castor sugar
1 egg yolk
675 g/1$\frac{1}{2}$ lb rhubarb
100 g/4 oz sugar
finely grated rind of 1 small orange
2 tablespoons orange juice
milk to glaze
castor sugar to sprinkle

Sift the flour and salt into a bowl. Cut the margarine and lard into pieces and rub into the flour with the fingertips until the mixture resembles fine breadcrumbs. Stir in the sugar, egg yolk and enough water to make a firm dough. Roll out half the pastry on a lightly floured board and use to line a deep 20-cm/8-inch pie plate.

Trim and chop the rhubarb and mix with the sugar, orange rind and juice. Turn into the lined pie plate. Damp the pastry edges with water.

Roll out the remaining pastry and use as a lid. Seal, flake and flute the edges. Roll out any trimmings and make into decorations. Brush all over with milk. Leave a hole in the centre for steam to escape. Sprinkle with sugar and cook in a moderately hot oven (200°C, 400°F, Gas Mark 6) for about 35 minutes.

Serve hot or cold. The pie can also be frozen. Store for up to 4 months.

Accompaniments
For a special occasion serve with zabaglione. Whisk 3 egg yolks in a bowl over hot water. Add 25 g/1 oz castor sugar and 2 tablespoons Marsala. Whisk until very thick and serve at once.

Plum Pie

Approximate preparation time: 25 minutes
Cooking time: 35 minutes
Serves 4–5

225 g/8 oz plain flour
pinch of salt
50 g/2 oz margarine
50 g/2 oz lard
450 g/1 lb Victoria plums
100 g/4 oz granulated sugar
pinch of ground mixed spice
egg to glaze

Sift the flour and salt into a bowl. Cut the margarine and lard into pieces and rub in with the fingertips until the mixture resembles fine breadcrumbs. Add cold water to make a fairly soft dough. Roll out half the pastry on a lightly floured board and use to line a 20-cm/8-inch pie plate.

Wash, halve and stone the plums. Place on the pastry-lined plate. Mix the sugar and spice and sprinkle over the plums. Damp the pastry edge with water. Roll out the remaining pastry and use as a lid. Seal the edges well and use the trimmings for decoration. Flake and flute the edges and brush all over with beaten egg. Make a hole in the centre for steam to escape.

Cook in a moderately hot oven (200°C, 400°F, Gas Mark 6) for about 35 minutes.

Serve hot or cold. If liked, the pie can be frozen for up to 6 months.

Pear and Orange Pie

Approximate preparation time: 30 minutes
Cooking time: 50 minutes
Serves 4–6

175 g/6 oz flour
pinch of salt
50 g/2 oz lard
50 g/2 oz margarine
225 g/8 oz granulated sugar
1 medium orange
1 small stick cinnamon
675 g/1½ lb firm pears
castor sugar to sprinkle

Sift the flour and salt into a bowl. Cut the lard and margarine into pieces and rub into the flour with the fingertips until the mixture resembles fine breadcrumbs. Add enough cold water to make a firm dough.

Put the sugar in a saucepan with 150 ml/¼ pint water. Heat gently to dissolve the sugar. Pare the zest from the orange, squeeze the juice and add to the syrup with the cinnamon stick. Boil for 5 minutes.

Meanwhile, peel, quarter and core the pears. Poach in the syrup for 10 minutes then drain.

Roll out the pastry to about 2.5-cm/1-inch larger than the diameter of a 20-cm/8-inch pie plate. Cut a 1-cm/½-inch strip from round the edge. Damp the strip. Line the plate with the pastry and mark the pastry rim with a fork. Arrange the pear quarters overlapping in the lined plate. Roll out the pastry trimmings, cut three 1-cm/½-inch strips and arrange across the pie. Damp and seal the ends. Cut out seven stars and place one at the ends of each strip and one in the centre.

Cook in a moderately hot oven (200°C, 400°F, Gas Mark 6) for 20 minutes. Reduce to moderate (180°C, 350°F, Gas Mark 4) for a further 10 minutes. Dredge with sugar and serve with cream or custard.

The pie can be frozen. Store for up to 4 months.

Dutch Plum Tart

Approximate preparation time: 25
minutes plus chilling time
Cooking time: 45–50 minutes
Serves 4

175 g/6 oz unsalted butter
50 g/2 oz castor sugar
50 g/2 oz ground almonds
grated rind of 1 small lemon
225 g/8 oz plain flour
675 g/1½ lb plums
100 g/4 oz granulated sugar
¼ teaspoon ground cinnamon
1 tablespoon icing sugar
red jam to glaze

Put the butter in a bowl with the sugar, almonds, lemon rind and 2 tablespoons of the flour. Beat until thoroughly mixed then add the remaining flour. If necessary add a little water to bind. Roll out two-thirds of the dough on a lightly floured surface and use to line a 20-cm/8-inch fluted flan ring. Prick the base all over with a fork.

Meanwhile put the plums in a saucepan with the sugar, cinnamon and about 150 ml/¼ pint water. Cook very gently for about 15 minutes or until tender. Drain and remove the stones.

Put the plums in the flan ring. Roll out the remaining pastry and cut out strips. Use these to make a lattice pattern over the plums, securing each end to the pastry rim with water.

Cook in a moderately hot oven (190°C, 375°F, Gas Mark 5) for 30–35 minutes. Sift the icing sugar over the top of the pastry. Heat the jam and brush over the plums. Serve hot with cream, ice cream or custard.

The tart may be frozen. Store for up to 4 months.

Prune and Apple Lattice Pies

Approximate preparation time: 25
minutes
Cooking time: 45–50 minutes
Serves 4

100 g/4 oz plain flour
pinch of salt
25 g/1 oz margarine
25 g/1 oz lard
225 g/8 oz prunes, soaked overnight
450 g/1 lb cooking apples
100 g/4 oz sugar
25 g/1 oz butter
1 tablespoon cornflour
2 tablespoons lemon juice
1 tablespoon grated lemon rind

Sift the flour and salt into a bowl. Cut the margarine and lard into pieces and rub into the flour with the fingertips until the mixture resembles fine breadcrumbs. Stir in enough cold water to make a firm dough.

Simmer the prunes in their soaking liquid for 10 minutes. Halve and remove the stones. Reserve the cooking liquid. Peel, core and slice the apples. Arrange the apples and prunes in four individual ovenproof dishes. Put 250 ml/8 fl oz of the cooking liquid in a saucepan with the sugar and butter. Heat gently to dissolve the sugar, then bring to the boil. Mix the cornflour with the lemon juice and stir into the liquid, stirring continuously. Stir in the lemon rind and divide equally between the dishes.

Roll out the pastry, cut out four strips and use to line the edges of the dishes. Roll out the rest and cut strips to make a lattice design on each dish. Secure the edges with water. Cook in a hot oven (230°C, 450°F, Gas Mark 5) for a further 20 minutes.

The pies can be frozen. Store for up to 4 months.

Apple and Cheese Pie

Approximate preparation time: 25
minutes
Cooking time: 30 minutes
Serves 4–6

225 g/8 oz plain flour
pinch of salt
50 g/2 oz margarine
50 g/2 oz lard
675 g/1½ lb cooking apples
175 g/6 oz Cheddar cheese
2 tablespoons castor sugar
1 egg
150 ml/¼ pint single cream

Sift the flour and salt into a bowl. Cut the margarine and lard into pieces and rub into the flour with the fingertips until the mixture resembles fine breadcrumbs. Stir in enough cold water to make a firm dough.

Roll out half the pastry on a lightly floured surface and use to line a 20-cm/8-inch pie plate.

Peel, core and slice the apples and grate the cheese. Spread half the apples over the pastry base and sprinkle with half the sugar and grated cheese. Cover with the remaining apple, sugar and cheese. Damp the pastry edges.

Roll out the remaining pastry and use as a lid. Seal the edges well. Flake and flute the edges, and brush all over with beaten egg. Cut slits in the top to allow the steam to escape. Cook in a moderately hot oven (200°C, 400°F, Gas Mark 6) for about 30 minutes.

Meanwhile warm the cream. When the pie is cooked, pour the cream in through the slits. Serve hot.

The pie can be frozen without the cream. Store for up to 4 months.

Apple Dumplings

Approximate preparation time: 25
minutes
Cooking time: 45–50 minutes
Serves 4

225 g/8 oz plain flour
pinch of salt
150 g/5 oz butter
4 medium dessert apples
3 teaspoons clear honey
1 egg
castor sugar to sprinkle

Grease a baking tray.

Sift the flour and salt into a bowl. Cut 100 g/4 oz of the butter in pieces and rub into the flour with the fingertips until the mixture resembles fine breadcrumbs. Mix in enough cold water to make a firm dough. Divide the dough into five equal pieces. Roll out four of the pieces into rounds big enough to enclose an apple.

Peel the apples and, keeping them whole, remove the cores to three-quarters of the way down. Fill the core cavities with honey and a knob of the remaining butter. Wrap the apples in the pastry. Beat the egg and brush over the pastry edges to seal them. Roll out the remaining pastry to make leaf shapes to decorate the apples. Place on the baking tray, brush all over with egg and cook in a hot oven (220°C, 425°F, Gas Mark 7) for 15 minutes. Reduce the heat to moderate (180°C, 350°F, Gas Mark 4) and cook for a further 30–35 minutes. Sprinkle with castor sugar.

These dumplings can be frozen. Store for up to 4 months.

Honey and Apple Flan

Approximate preparation time: 20 minutes
Cooking time: 30–35 minutes
Serves 6

350 g/12 oz plain flour
pinch of salt
75 g/3 oz margarine
75 g/3 oz lard
900 g/2 lb cooking apples
2 tablespoons clear honey
25 g/1 oz soft brown sugar
25 g/1 oz butter
25 g/1 oz plain flour
$\frac{1}{4}$ teaspoon ground cinnamon
milk to glaze
castor sugar to sprinkle

Sift the flour and salt into a bowl. Cut the margarine and lard into pieces and rub into the flour with the fingertips until the mixture resembles fine breadcrumbs. Add enough cold water to make a firm dough. Roll out two-thirds of the pastry on a lightly floured surface and use to line a 20-cm/8-inch fluted flan ring. Prick the base with a fork.

Peel, core and slice the apples and arrange in the flan in overlapping layers. Mix the honey, sugar and butter together. Sift the flour and cinnamon and stir into the honey mixture. Spread over the apples.

Roll out the remaining pastry and cut into long 1-cm/$\frac{1}{2}$-inch wide strips. Arrange these in a lattice pattern on the flan, securing the ends with milk.

Brush all the pastry with milk and cook in a moderately hot oven (200°C, 400°F, Gas Mark 6) for 30–35 minutes. Sprinkle with the castor sugar.

This can be frozen. Store for up to 4 months.

Mincemeat Tart

Approximate preparation time: 15 minutes
Cooking time: 30 minutes
Serves 4

175 g/6 oz plain flour
pinch of salt
40 g/1$\frac{1}{2}$ oz margarine
40 g/1$\frac{1}{2}$ oz lard
1 small cooking apple
juice of $\frac{1}{2}$ small lemon
8 tablespoons mincemeat

Sift the flour and salt into a bowl. Cut the margarine and lard into pieces and rub into the flour with the fingertips until the mixture resembles fine breadcrumbs. Stir in enough cold water to make a firm dough. Roll out the pastry on a lightly floured surface and use to line a 20-cm/8-inch fluted flan ring or dish. Prick the base with a fork.

Peel, core and grate the apple. Mix with the lemon juice and mincemeat and spoon into the flan. Cook in a moderately hot oven (200°C, 400°F, Gas Mark 6) for about 30 minutes.

This can be frozen. Store for up to 4 months.

Accompaniments
Either serve with cream or with a sweet white sauce. Melt 20 g/$\frac{3}{4}$ oz butter in a saucepan. Stir in 20 g/$\frac{3}{4}$ oz flour and cook, stirring for 2 minutes. Gradually add 300 ml/$\frac{1}{2}$ pint milk and bring to the boil, stirring. Cook for 2 minutes and sweeten with 20 g/$\frac{3}{4}$ oz sugar.

Gooseberry Cake

Approximate preparation time: 15
minutes
Cooking time: 35 minutes
Serves 4–6

**1 (212-g/7½-oz) packet frozen
shortcrust pastry, thawed
1 (425-g/15-oz) can gooseberries
pinch of ground mixed spice
75 g/3 oz fresh white breadcrumbs
65 g/2½ oz granulated sugar**

Lightly grease an 18-cm/7-inch fluted flan tin.

Roll out the pastry on a lightly floured surface and use to line the flan tin.

Drain the gooseberries. (In summer use fresh ones, stewed, drained and sweetened). Mix in the spice, breadcrumbs and 50 g/2 oz of the sugar. Spoon into the lined tin.

Cook in a moderately hot oven (200°C, 400°F, Gas Mark 6) for about 35 minutes. Sprinkle with the remaining sugar and leave to cool.

Eat the same day, or freeze and store for up to 4 months.

Fresh Fruit Flan

Approximate preparation time: 20
minutes
Cooking time: 20 minutes
Serves 4

**100 g/4 oz plain flour
pinch of salt
50 g/2 oz butter
1 large and 1 small orange
1 large banana
100 g/4 oz black grapes
1–2 tablespoons apricot jam
150 ml/¼ pint double cream**

Lightly grease a 20-cm/8-inch flan tin.

Sift the flour and salt into a bowl. Cut the butter in pieces and rub into the flour with the fingertips until the mixture resembles fine breadcrumbs. Add enough cold water to make a firm dough. Roll out the pastry on a lightly floured surface and use to line the prepared tin. Prick the base with a fork. Bake blind in a moderately hot oven (200°C, 400°F, Gas Mark 6) for about 20 minutes. Leave to cool completely.

Peel the large orange, removing all the pith and divide the flesh into segments. Squeeze the juice from the small orange and peel and slice the banana. Toss the banana slices in the orange juice.

Heat the jam with 2 tablespoons water until it melts. Whip the cream and spread over the base of the flan and arrange the fruit on top. Brush the fruit with the hot jam.

Eat the same day.

Grape Flan

Approximate preparation time: 25
minutes
Cooking time: 20 minutes
Serves 4

**100 g/4 oz plain flour
pinch of salt
50 g/2 oz butter
150 ml/¼ pint cold thick custard
150 ml/¼ pint double cream
1 tablespoon apricot brandy
175 g/6 oz green grapes
175 g/6 oz black grapes**

Lightly grease a 20-cm/8-inch flan ring or dish.

Sift the flour and salt into a bowl. Cut the butter in pieces and rub into the flour with the fingertips until the mixture resembles fine breadcrumbs. Stir in enough cold water to make a stiff dough. Roll out the pastry on a lightly floured surface and use to line the prepared flan ring or dish. Prick the base with a fork and bake blind in a moderately hot oven (200°C, 400°F, Gas Mark 6) for about 20 minutes. Leave to cool completely.

Mix the custard with the cream and apricot brandy. Spoon into the cold flan. Remove the pips from the grapes then arrange in a pattern on the cream.

Serve within 4 hours.

Summer Flan

Approximate preparation time: 20
minutes
Cooking time: 20 minutes
Serves 3–4

100 g/4 oz plain flour
pinch of salt
50 g/2 oz butter or margarine
150 ml/$\frac{1}{4}$ pint double or canned
cream
2 teaspoons chopped mint
450 g/1 lb raspberries

Lightly grease a 20-cm/8-inch flan tin or dish.

Sift the flour and salt into a bowl. Cut the butter or margarine in pieces and rub into the flour with the fingertips until the mixture resembles fine breadcrumbs. Stir in enough water to make a firm dough. Roll out the pastry on a lightly floured surface and use to line the prepared flan dish. Prick the base with a fork and bake blind in a moderately hot oven (200°C, 400°F, Gas Mark 6) for about 20 minutes. Leave to cool completely.

Mix the mint into the cream and spread over the base of the flan. Arrange the raspberries on top.

Serve within 4 hours.

Variations
The mint flavoured cream goes well with strawberries or blackberries too. For a special occasion, pipe some whipped cream on the top to decorate. Decorate with a few mint leaves or finely grated orange rind.

Strawberry Fluff Flan

Approximate preparation time: 25
minutes
Cooking time: 30 minutes
Serves 4

100 g/4 oz plain flour
pinch of salt
50 g/2 oz hard butter
175 g/6 oz raspberries
225 g/8 oz strawberries
75 g/3 oz castor sugar
1 large egg white

Lightly grease a 20-cm/8-inch flan tin or dish.

Sift the flour and salt into a bowl. Cut the butter in pieces and rub into the flour with the fingertips until the mixture resembles fine breadcrumbs. Stir in enough cold water to make a firm dough. Roll out the pastry on a lightly floured surface and use to line the prepared flan tin. Prick the base with a fork and bake blind in a moderately hot oven (200°C, 400°F, Gas Mark 6) for 15 minutes. Leave to cool completely.

Put the raspberries and 175 g/6 oz of the strawberries in the flan and sprinkle with 25 g/1 oz of the sugar. Whisk the egg white until very stiff and standing in peaks. Whisk in the remaining sugar. Pile over the fruit and cook in a moderately hot oven (200°C, 400°F, Gas Mark 6) until crisp outside. Cool and decorate with the remaining strawberries.

Serve within 4 hours with cream.

American Summer Pie

Approximate preparation time: 25 minutes
Cooking time: 20 minutes
Serves 4

100 g/4 oz plain flour
50 g/2 oz butter
300 ml/½ pint double cream
4 tablespoons single cream
2 teaspoons orange milk-shake syrup
few roasted pecan nuts or toasted almonds

Sift the flour into a bowl. Cut the butter in pieces and rub into the flour with the fingertips until the mixture resembles fine breadcrumbs. Stir in enough cold water to make a firm dough. Roll out the pastry on a lightly floured surface and use to line a 20-cm/8-inch pie plate. Prick all over with a fork and bake blind in a moderately hot oven (200°C, 400°F, Gas Mark 6) for 20 minutes. Leave to cool completely.

Whisk the double and single creams together with the orange syrup. Turn into the pastry case. Decorate with the pecans or almonds.

Serve within 4 hours.

Variations

Different milk-shake syrup flavours can be used, or for a sharper flavour use natural yogurt instead of single cream.

For a more elaborate dessert, put a layer of apple purée or some slices of sweet red-skinned apple, in the flan before adding the cream.

Lemon Meringue Pie

Approximate preparation time: 20 minutes
Cooking time: 1 hour 10 minutes
Serves 4

1 (212-g/7½-oz) packet frozen shortcrust pastry, thawed
grated rind of 1 and juice of 2 lemons
25 g/1 oz cornflour
225 g/8 oz castor sugar
15 g/½ oz butter
2 large eggs, separated

Lightly grease a 20-cm/8-inch flan tin.

Roll out the pastry on a lightly floured surface and use to line the prepared tin. Prick the pastry with a fork and bake blind in a moderately hot oven (200°C, 400°F, Gas Mark 6) for 20 minutes. Leave to cool completely.

Mix the lemon juice with the cornflour and stir in 300 ml/½ pint boiling water. Simmer for 2 minutes then beat in half the sugar, the butter and lemon rind. Beat in the egg yolks and pour into the flan.

Whisk the egg whites until very stiff and standing in peaks. Whisk in the remaining sugar a little at a time. Pile the meringue over the lemon mixture. Cook in a cool oven (150°C, 300°F, Gas Mark 2) for 40–50 minutes. Cool completely.

Eat the same day for this pie to be at its best.

Apricot Chiffon Flan

Approximate preparation time: 30 minutes (plus standing time)
Cooking time: 20 minutes
Serves 4–5

175 g/6 oz plain flour
pinch of salt
75 g/3 oz lard
15 g/$\frac{1}{2}$ oz powdered gelatine
pared rind and juice of 1 medium orange
1 (425-g/15-oz) can apricot halves
50 g/2 oz castor sugar
2 standard eggs, separated
150 ml/$\frac{1}{4}$ pint double cream
few drops orange colouring

Lightly grease a 20-cm/8-inch sandwich tin.

Sift the flour and salt into a bowl. Cut the lard in pieces and rub in with the fingertips until the mixture resembles fine bread-crumbs. Stir in enough cold water to make a firm dough. Roll out the pastry on a lightly floured surface and use to line the prepared tin. Prick the base with a fork and bake blind in a moderately hot oven (200°C, 400°F, Gas Mark 6) for about 20 minutes. Leave to cool.

Dissolve the gelatine in 4 tablespoons water in a small bowl over hot water.

Cut the orange rind in very thin shreds. Sieve or liquidise the apricots with their syrup. Put the sugar in a bowl and beat with the egg yolks until thick and frothy. Beat in the gelatine, apricot purée and orange juice. Whisk the egg whites until very stiff and standing in peaks. Fold into the fruit mixture. Whip the cream and fold in with a few drops of colouring. Pour into the pastry case and leave in a cool place to set.

Eat the same day.

Sweetheart Lemon Flan

Approximate preparation time: 25 minutes
Cooking time: 30 minutes
Serves 4

175 g/6 oz plain flour
pinch of salt
40 g/1$\frac{1}{2}$ oz margarine
40 g/1$\frac{1}{2}$ oz lard
100 g/4 oz butter
100 g/4 oz castor sugar
100 g/4 oz semolina
$\frac{1}{2}$ teaspoon almond essence
grated rind of 1 small lemon
1 egg
2 tablespoons apricot jam
15 g/$\frac{1}{2}$ oz icing sugar

Sift the flour and salt into a bowl. Cut the margarine and lard in pieces and rub into the flour with the fingertips until the mixture resembles fine breadcrumbs. Stir in enough cold water to make a firm dough. Roll out the pastry on a lightly floured board and use to line a 20-cm/8-inch flan ring. Reserve the trimmings and prick the base of the flan with a fork.

Melt the butter and stir in the sugar. Cook for 1 minute. Stir in the semolina, almond essence and lemon rind and remove from the heat. Remove 2 teaspoons of the egg white and reserve. Beat the remaining egg and stir into the semolina mixture. Spread the jam over the pastry base and cover with the filling mixture.

Sift the icing sugar, beat in the reserved egg white and brush carefully over the filling. Roll out the pastry trimmings and cut in heart shapes. Use these to decorate the flan. Cook in a moderately hot oven (200°C, 400°F, Gas Mark 6) for about 30 minutes.

The flan can be frozen. Store for up to 4 months and thaw for 4–5 hours.

Lemon Honey Flan

Approximate preparation time: 20
minutes
Cooking time: 30 minutes
Serves 4

175 g/6 oz plain flour
pinch of salt
75 g/3 oz hard butter
25 g/1 oz cornflour
300 ml/$\frac{1}{2}$ pint milk
2 tablespoons clear honey
2 tablespoons lemon juice
few drops yellow colouring
40 g/1$\frac{1}{2}$ oz margarine
4 tablespoons top of the milk
25 g/1 oz soft brown sugar
2 small lemons
angelica for decoration

Sift the flour and salt into a bowl. Cut the butter in pieces and rub in with the finger-tips until the mixture resembles fine bread-crumbs. Stir in enough cold water to make a firm dough. Roll out the pastry on a lightly floured surface and use to line a 23-cm/9-inch flan dish or tin. Prick the base with a fork and bake blind in a moderately hot oven (200°C, 400°F, Gas Mark 6) for about 20 minutes.

Mix the cornflour with a little of the milk until smooth. Bring the remaining milk to the boil and mix into the cornflour. Pour back into the pan and add the honey and lemon juice. Add a few drops of colouring and 15 g/$\frac{1}{2}$ oz of the margarine. Simmer, stirring for 3 minutes. Stir in the top of the milk and pour into the flan. Leave to cool.

Heat the remaining margarine in a frying pan. Sprinkle in the sugar. Slice the lemons thinly and fry gently until just coloured. Cool, then use to decorate the flan with the angelica.

Eat within 4 hours.

Apple Bakewell Tart

Approximate preparation time: 25 minutes
Cooking time: 20–30 minutes
Serves 4–5

100 g/4 oz plain flour
pinch of salt
50 g/2 oz margarine
1½ tablespoons raspberry jam
50 g/2 oz butter
50 g/2 oz castor sugar
1 large egg
grated rind of ½ lemon
75 g/3 oz cake crumbs, sieved
75 g/3 oz ground almonds
thin slices of cooking apple

Sift the flour and salt into a bowl. Cut the margarine in pieces and rub into the flour with the fingertips until the mixture resembles fine breadcrumbs. Stir in enough cold water to make a firm dough. Roll out the pastry on a lightly floured board and use to line a 20-cm/8-inch loose-based flan tin.

Spread the jam over the pastry base. Cream the butter and sugar until light and fluffy. Beat the egg and add gradually to the creamed mixture with the lemon rind. Mix the crumbs and almonds and fold half into the mixture. Stir in the remainder. Spread the mixture over the jam, smooth the top and cook in a moderately hot oven (200°C, 400°F, Gas Mark 6) for 15 minutes. Reduce the oven to moderate (180°C, 350°F, Gas Mark 4), add the sliced apple and cook for a further 20–30 minutes.

Eat the same day or freeze. Store for up to 4 months.

Variations
If liked, add a few drops of almond essence to the uncooked filling. For a special occasion, pipe cream around the edge and sprinkle with grated chocolate.

Norwegian Almond Tart

Approximate preparation time: 25
minutes
Cooking time: 45 minutes
Serves 6

150 g/5 oz plain flour
pinch of salt
65 g/2½ oz butter
65 g/2½ oz castor sugar
2 eggs
100 g/4 oz ground almonds
100 g/4 oz icing sugar
few drops almond essence
icing sugar to dust

Sift the flour and salt into a bowl. Cut the butter in pieces and rub into the flour with the fingertips until the mixture resembles fine breadcrumbs. Stir in the sugar. Beat one egg and mix in to form a firm dough. Add a little water if necessary. Roll out the pastry on a lightly floured surface and use to line a 23-cm/9-inch fluted flan dish or tin. Prick the base with a fork. Roll out the pastry trimmings and cut in long strips. Separate the second egg. Mix the yolk with the ground almonds, icing sugar and almond essence. Whisk the egg white until stiff and standing in peaks and fold into the yolk mixture with a metal spoon. Turn the mixture into the flan and make a lattice over the top, twisting the pastry strips and sealing the ends with water. Cook in a hot oven (220°C, 425°F, Gas Mark 7) for 15 minutes. Reduce the oven to cool (150°C, 300°F, Gas Mark 2) for a further 30 minutes. Sift the icing sugar over the top and serve with ice cream or cream.

This flan can be frozen. Store for up to 4 months.

Almond Swiss Flan

Approximate preparation time: 25
minutes
Cooking time: 35 minutes
Serves 4

200 g/7 oz plain flour
pinch of salt
150 g/5 oz butter
50 g/2 oz castor sugar
1 large egg
few drops almond essence
25 g/1 oz ground almonds
3 tablespoons raspberry jam, or use
raspberry jam flavoured with
liqueur
50 g/2 oz icing sugar
1 (113-g/4-oz) jar red cocktail
cherries, or use fresh stoned
cherries

Sift 175 g/6 oz of the flour and the salt into a bowl. Cut 75 g/3 oz of the butter in pieces and rub into the flour with the fingertips until the mixture resembles fine breadcrumbs. Stir in enough cold water to make a firm dough. Roll out the pastry on a lightly floured surface and use to line an 18-cm/7-inch flan dish or tin. Prick the base with a fork.

Cream the remaining butter with the sugar until light and fluffy. Beat in the egg and almond essence. Fold in the remaining flour and ground almonds.

Spread the jam over the pastry base and spread the almond mixture over the top. Cook in a moderately hot oven (200°C, 400°F, Gas Mark 6) for a further 30 minutes. Leave to cool.

Sift the icing sugar and mix in enough water to make a piping consistency. Fit a piping bag with a medium star nozzle and fill the bag with the icing. Pipe swirls on the flan and decorate with the cherries.

Eat the same day or freeze without the decorations. Store for up to 4 months.

Yogurt Tarts

Approximate preparation time: 20
minutes
Cooking time: 10 minutes
Serves 5

90 g/3½ oz plain flour
50 g/2 oz butter
1 tablespoon castor sugar
1 small egg yolk
1 (142-ml/5-fl oz) carton raspberry
yogurt
50 g/2 oz cream cheese
few large strawberries with the
stalks left on

Sift the flour into a bowl. Cut the butter in pieces and rub into the flour with the fingertips until the mixture resembles fine breadcrumbs. Mix in the sugar, egg yolk and enough cold water to make a firm dough. Roll out the pastry on a lightly floured surface and use to line five tartlet tins. Prick the bases with a fork and bake blind in a moderately hot oven (200°C, 400°F, Gas Mark 6) for about 10 minutes. Cool on a wire rack.

Mix the yogurt with the cream cheese and use to fill the cases. Decorate with the strawberries.

Eat the same day.

Variation
For a sharper flavour, mix the cream cheese with natural yogurt.

Traditional Cheesecake

Approximate preparation time: 25
minutes
Cooking time: 30 minutes
Serves 4–5

150 g/5 oz plain flour
pinch of salt
75 g/3 oz butter or margarine
2 large eggs plus 1 egg yolk
grated rind and juice of 1 small
lemon
225 g/8 oz cream cheese
50 g/2 oz castor sugar
50 g/2 oz sultanas
a few canned or fresh peach slices

Lightly grease a 20-cm/8-inch sandwich tin or loose-bottomed flan tin.

Sift the flour and salt into a mixing bowl. Cut the butter or margarine in pieces and rub into the flour until the mixture resembles fine breadcrumbs. Mix in the egg yolk and enough cold water to make a firm dough. Roll out the pastry on a lightly floured surface and use to line the prepared tin. Reserve the pastry trimmings.

Separate the eggs and mix the yolks well with the lemon rind, juice, cream cheese, sugar and sultanas.

Whisk the egg whites until very stiff and standing in peaks. Fold into the cream cheese mixture with a metal spoon and turn out into the pastry case. Reroll the pastry trimmings and cut fine, narrow strips. Arrange these in a lattice pattern over the filling. Cook in a moderately hot oven (200°C, 400°F, Gas Mark 6) for about 30 minutes. Leave to cool.

Decorate the cooked cheesecake with the peach slices.

Eat the same day, or freeze and store for up to 2 months.

Blackcurrant Cheesecake

Approximate preparation time: 25 minutes
Cooking time: 1 hour 20 minutes
Serves 4–6

175 g/6 oz plain flour
75 g/3 oz butter, chilled
40 g/1½ oz butter, softened
40 g/1½ oz castor sugar
1 large egg, separated
2 teaspoons custard powder
100 g/4 oz curd cheese
1 teaspoon lemon juice
grated rind and juice of ½ orange
450 g/1 lb blackcurrants, cooked
and sweetened
few raw blackcurrants to decorate

Sift the flour into a bowl and rub in the chilled butter until the mixture resembles fine breadcrumbs. Mix in 6 teaspoons cold water and mix to a firm dough. Roll out the pastry on a lightly floured surface and use to line an 18-cm/7-inch loose-bottomed cake tin. Prick the pastry all over and cook in a moderately hot oven (200°C, 400°F, Gas Mark 6) for 20 minutes or until golden.

Cream the softened butter with the sugar until light and creamy. Beat the egg yolk into the creamed mixture and stir in the custard powder, cheese and lemon juice. Add the orange rind and juice to the cheese mixture. Whisk the egg white until stiff and fold into the mixture using a metal spoon. Spread the cooked blackcurrants over the pastry. Turn the cheese mixture into the case over the fruit. Cook in a moderate oven (160°C, 325°F, Gas Mark 3) for 50 minutes. Turn the oven off and leave the cheesecake in the cooling oven for a further 10 minutes or until firm. Leave to cool. Decorate with the reserved blackcurrants.

Variations
Instead of using blackcurrants, try canned cherries or apricots, puréed cooked apples or pears, black grapes or chocolate curls.

Cherry Cheesecake

Approximate preparation time: 25 minutes
Cooking time: 1 hour 40 minutes
Serves 4–6

1 (370-g/13-oz) packet frozen
shortcrust pastry, thawed
40 g/1½ oz butter
40 g/1½ oz castor sugar
1 teaspoon custard powder
1 large egg, separated
100 g/4 oz curd cheese
1 teaspoon lemon juice
1 small orange
1 (396-g/14-oz) can cherry pie filling

Roll out the pastry on a lightly floured surface and use to line an 18-cm/7-inch loose-bottomed cake tin. Prick the base of the pastry with a fork. Bake blind in a moderately hot oven (200°C, 400°F, Gas Mark 6) for 25 minutes or until crisp and golden.

Cream the butter and sugar together until light and fluffy and beat in the custard powder and egg yolk. Stir in the cheese and lemon juice. Halve the orange and grate the rind and squeeze the juice from half of it. Add the rind and juice to the mixture.

Whisk the egg white until stiff then fold into the cheese mixture using a metal spoon. Turn into the cold pastry case and cook in a moderate oven (160°C, 325°F, Gas Mark 3) for 50 minutes. Turn the oven off and leave the cheesecake in the oven with the door open for 20 minutes. Leave to cool completely. Spread the pie filling over the top of the cheesecake and decorate with the rest of the orange, cut in slices.

Blackcurrant Cheesecake

HOT PUDDINGS

Ginger Pudding

Approximate preparation time: 25 minutes
Cooking time: $1\frac{1}{2}$ hours
Serves 4–6

6 tablespoons lemon curd
100 g/4 oz butter
100 g/4 oz castor sugar
2 eggs
175 g/6 oz self-raising flour
75 g/3 oz stem ginger, chopped
2–3 tablespoons milk
toasted chopped almonds to decorate

Half fill a large saucepan or steamer with water and bring to the boil. Grease a 1-litre/$1\frac{1}{2}$-pint basin.

Put 4 tablespoons of the lemon curd in the bottom of the basin. Cream the butter and sugar together until light and fluffy. Beat the eggs and add gradually to the creamed mixture, beating well. Sift the flour over the top and fold in with the ginger using a metal spoon. Add enough milk to produce a soft, dropping consistency. Turn the mixture into the prepared basin and cover tightly with greased greaseproof paper and foil. Steam for $1\frac{1}{2}$ hours, checking the water level from time to time. Turn out and sprinkle with the chopped nuts. Heat the remaining lemon curd and use as a sauce.

Serve immediately.

Chocolate Pudding

Approximate preparation time: 15 minutes
Cooking time: 2 hours
Serves 4–6

175 g/6 oz margarine
175 g/6 oz castor sugar
3 eggs
200 g/7 oz self-raising flour
25 g/1 oz cocoa
$\frac{1}{2}$ teaspoon baking powder
100 g/4 oz plain chocolate
15 g/$\frac{1}{2}$ oz cornflour

Half fill a large saucepan or steamer with water and bring to the boil. Grease a 1-litre/$1\frac{1}{2}$-pint pudding basin.

Cream the margarine and sugar together until light and fluffy. Beat the eggs and add gradually to the creamed mixture. Sift the flour, cocoa and baking powder over the top and fold in with a metal spoon. Turn the mixture into the prepared basin and cover tightly with greased greaseproof paper and foil. Steam for about 2 hours.

Break up the chocolate and place in a bowl over a pan of hot water. Add 200 ml/7 fl oz water and melt until smooth. Mix the cornflour with 4 tablespoons water and stir into the chocolate mixture. Transfer to a saucepan and heat, stirring, until thick. Turn out the pudding.

Serve immediately with the sauce.

Steamed Jam Pudding

Approximate preparation time: 15 minutes
Cooking time: 2 hours
Serves 4–6

175 g/6 oz margarine
175 g/6 oz castor sugar
3 eggs
225 g/8 oz self-raising flour
100 g/4 oz raspberry jam

Half fill a large saucepan or steamer with water and bring to the boil. Grease a 1.25-litre/2-pint pudding basin.

Cream the margarine and sugar together until light and fluffy. Beat the eggs and add gradually to the creamed mixture. Sift the flour over the top and fold in with a metal spoon. Turn the mixture into the prepared basin and cover tightly with greased greaseproof paper and foil. Steam for 2 hours. Heat the raspberry jam.

Serve immediately with the jam as a sauce.

Spiced Fruit Pudding

Approximate preparation time: 20 minutes
Cooking time: 2 hours
Serves 4–6

175 g/6 oz margarine
175 g/6 oz castor sugar
3 eggs
225 g/8 oz self-raising flour
$\frac{1}{2}$ teaspoon ground mixed spice
75 g/3 oz currants
75 g/3 oz sultanas
50 g/2 oz chopped mixed peel

Half fill a large saucepan or steamer with water and bring to the boil. Grease a 1.25-litre/2-pint pudding basin.

Cream the margarine and sugar until light and fluffy. Beat the eggs and add gradually to the creamed mixture. Sift the flour and spice over the top and fold in with a metal spoon. Stir in the currants, sultanas and peel. Turn the mixture into the prepared basin and cover tightly with greased greaseproof paper and foil. Steam for 2 hours. Turn out and serve immediately with custard.

Variation
Serve the pudding with a syrup sauce. Put 5 tablespoons golden syrup in a saucepan with 4 tablespoons water and the strained juice of half an orange. Heat until the syrup melts.

Spotted Dick

Approximate preparation time: 20 minutes
Cooking time: 3 hours
Serves 4–6

225 g/8 oz self-raising flour
pinch of salt
1 teaspoon baking powder
100 g/4 oz shredded suet
75 g/3 oz castor sugar
75 g/3 oz currants
75 g/3 oz sultanas
1–2 tablespoons milk

Half fill a large saucepan or steamer with water and bring to the boil.

Sprinkle a little flour on a clean cloth.

Sift the flour, salt and baking powder together. Stir in the suet, sugar, currants and sultanas. Add enough milk to produce a soft dough. Shape into a roll and place on the prepared cloth. Fold over the ends of the cloth and tie the ends. Steam for 3 hours.

Serve at once with custard or hot golden syrup.

Christmas Pudding

Approximate preparation time: 30
minutes
Cooking time: 6 hours (plus reheating)
Serves 4–6

100 g/4 oz chilled butter
300 g/11 oz currants
25 g/1 oz blanched almonds,
chopped
300 g/11 oz raisins
100 g/4 oz fresh white breadcrumbs
50 g/2 oz clear honey
25 g/1 oz plain flour
3 eggs
grated rind of 1 large lemon
holly for decoration

Make at least 2 weeks before Christmas and store in the refrigerator.

Boil a large plain cotton rectangle for 2 minutes and wring out well. Fold in half to make an approximately 60-cm/24-inch square. Grease the cloth with lard and put a large piece of greaseproof paper in the centre.

Grate the butter and mix with all the other ingredients. Turn the pudding mixture on to the paper and shape into a neat round. Mould the paper around the pudding, bring the corners of the cloth together and tie securely with string.

Fold a tea cloth and place in a pan of boiling water. This prevents burning. Lower the pudding into the water so it is completely submerged. Cover and boil for 6 hours, topping up the water when necessary. When cooked, unwrap, cool and wrap in greaseproof paper and foil.

Store in the refrigerator.

Cherry-topped Almond Pudding

Approximate preparation time: 15
minutes
Cooking time: 2 hours
Serves 4–6

50 g/2 oz blanched almonds
175 g/6 oz margarine
175 g/6 oz castor sugar
3 eggs
$\frac{1}{2}$ **teaspoon almond essence**
225 g/8 oz self-raising flour
50 g/2 oz glacé cherries
1 (213-g/7$\frac{1}{2}$-oz) can cherries
2 teaspoons arrowroot

Half fill a large saucepan or steamer with
water and bring to the boil. Grease a 1.25-
litre/2-pint pudding basin.

Chop the nuts finely. Cream the margarine and sugar together until light and
fluffy. Beat the eggs and add gradually to
the creamed mixture. Beat in the almond
essence. Sift the flour over the top and fold
in with a metal spoon. Chop the glacé
cherries and stir into the mixture with the
almonds. Turn the mixture into the prepared
basin and cover tightly with greased
greaseproof paper and foil. Steam for 2
hours, topping up the water as necessary.

About 5 minutes before the end of cooking time, mix the juice from the can of
cherries with the arrowroot and bring to the
boil, stirring continuously. Simmer for 2
minutes. Mix in the cherries.

Turn out the pudding and serve immediately with the cherries and juice poured
on top.

Fruit Pudding with Butter Orange Sauce

Approximate preparation time: 20
minutes
Cooking time: 2 hours
Serves 6

225 g/8 oz self-raising flour
175 g/6 oz butter
100 g/4 oz castor sugar
75 g/3 oz sultanas
2 eggs
3 tablespoons milk
pared rind and juice of 1 medium
orange
50 g/2 oz granulated sugar

Grease a 15-cm/6-inch cake tin or a 1.25-litre/2-pint pudding basin. Half fill a large saucepan or steamer with water and bring to the boil.

Sift the flour into a bowl and rub in 100 g/4 oz of the butter with the fingertips until the mixture resembles fine breadcrumbs. Stir in the sugar and sultanas. Mix with the eggs and enough milk to make a fairly soft mixture. Turn into the prepared tin or basin and cover securely with greased greaseproof paper and foil. Steam for 2 hours.

For the sauce, put the orange rind in a saucepan and make the juice up to 300 ml/$\frac{1}{2}$ pint with water. Pour into the pan, add the sugar and heat until the sugar has dissolved. Boil until the mixture is syrupy and is reduced to about 150 ml/$\frac{1}{4}$ pint. Lift out and reserve the rind.

Turn out the pudding and pour over the sauce. Decorate with the orange rind.

Serve immediately. Left-over pudding can be reheated in a covered dish in a moderate oven (180°C, 350°F, Gas Mark 4) for 20 minutes.

Orange Pudding

Approximate preparation time: 15
minutes
Cooking time: 2 hours
Serves 4–6

175 g/6 oz margarine
175 g/6 oz castor sugar
3 eggs
grated rind and juice of 1 small
orange
250 g/9 oz self-raising flour
slices of orange to decorate

Half fill a large saucepan or steamer with water and bring to the boil. Grease a 1.25-litre/2-pint pudding basin.

Cream the margarine and sugar together until light and fluffy. Beat the eggs and add gradually to the creamed mixture. Beat in the orange rind and juice. Sift the flour over the top and fold in with a metal spoon.

Turn the mixture into the prepared basin and cover securely with greased greaseproof paper and foil. Steam for 2 hours.

Turn out the pudding and decorate with slices of orange.

Serve immediately with cream or custard.

Variations

For a stronger flavour, use a lemon instead of the orange and soft brown sugar to replace the castor.

Serve with plain or sweetened natural yogurt or with cherry or apricot pie filling heated and used as a sauce. Stewed puréed apples, sweetened and spiced with cinnamon and sultanas makes an unusual sauce.

Apple and Lemon Pudding

Approximate preparation time: 15 minutes
Cooking time: 2–2½ hours
Serves 6–8

1 medium cooking apple
150 ml/¼ pint golden syrup
100 g/4 oz plain flour
1½ teaspoons baking powder
½ teaspoon salt
½ teaspoon ground cinnamon
grated rind and juice of 1 small lemon
100 g/4 oz fresh white breadcrumbs
75 g/3 oz currants
75 g/3 oz shredded suet
100 g/4 oz castor sugar
1 egg
1–2 tablespoons milk

Grease 1.5-litre/2½-pint pudding basin. Half fill a large saucepan or steamer with water and bring to the boil.

Core the apple and slice in half crossways. Cut a thin slice of apple and place in the bottom of the prepared basin. Put half the golden syrup on top.

Sift the flour into a bowl with the baking powder, salt and cinnamon. Add the lemon rind, breadcrumbs, currants, suet and sugar. Finely chop the remaining apple and add to the mixture. Beat the egg with the milk and stir into the mixture to make a soft dough. Turn into the prepared basin and cover securely with greased greaseproof paper and foil. Steam for 2–2½ hours.

Mix the remaining syrup with the lemon juice.

Turn out the pudding and serve immediately with the syrup sauce.

Walnut Pudding

Approximate preparation time: 15 minutes
Cooking time: 2 hours
Serves 4–6

175 g/6 oz margarine
175 g/6 oz brown sugar
3 eggs
50 g/2 oz finely ground walnuts
225 g/8 oz self-raising flour
1–2 tablespoons milk
100 g/4 oz plain chocolate
15 g/½ oz cornflour

Half fill a large saucepan or steamer with water and bring to the boil. Grease a 1.25-litre/2-pint pudding basin.

Cream the margarine and sugar until light and fluffy. Beat the eggs and add gradually to the creamed mixture. Sift the flour over the top and fold in with the walnuts using a metal spoon. Add enough milk to make a soft dropping consistency. Turn into the prepared basin, cover securely with greased greaseproof paper and foil and steam for 2 hours.

To make the sauce, melt the chocolate with 200 ml/7 fl oz water in a small bowl over a pan of hot water. Mix the cornflour with 4 tablespoons water and stir into the chocolate. Transfer to a small saucepan and cook for 3 minutes, stirring.

Turn out the pudding and serve immediately with the sauce.

Variations
Instead of chocolate sauce, serve the pudding with a rhubarb compote. Cut 450 g/1 lb rhubarb in 5-cm/2-inch lengths and simmer with 50 g/2 oz sugar and a little water until tender. If liked, use orange juice instead of water.

Apple Upside Down Tart

Approximate preparation time: 35 minutes
Cooking time: 35–45 minutes
Serves 4

100 g/4 oz granulated sugar
2 tablespoons water
900 g/2 lb dessert apples
100 g/4 oz plain flour
pinch of salt
25 g/1 oz margarine
25 g/1 oz lard

Grease the sides only of a 20-cm/8-inch cake tin.

Put the sugar and water in a small pan.

Heat to dissolve the sugar then increase the heat and boil, without stirring, until the mixture is a rich caramel colour. Pour into the cake tin.

Peel, quarter and core the apples. Slice thinly and arrange in an overlapping pattern over the base of the tin. Add the rest of the apple to make an even layer.

Sift the flour and salt together, cut the margarine in pieces and rub in with the fingertips until the mixture resembles fine breadcrumbs. Stir in enough cold water to make a firm dough. Roll out on a lightly floured board to fit the size of the tin. Place on top of the apple layer and prick all over with a fork. Cook in a moderately hot oven (200°C, 400°F, Gas Mark 6) for 30–40 minutes. Remove from the oven, cool for a few minutes then, using a heatproof plate over the tart, invert the tin and allow the caramel to run down.

Serve at once with cream.

Pineapple Upside Down Pudding

Approximate preparation time: 25 minutes
Cooking time: 30–40 minutes
Serves 4

150 g/5 oz butter
150 g/5 oz soft brown sugar
1 (376-g/13$\frac{1}{4}$-oz) can pineapple rings
4 glacé cherries
7 walnut halves
2 eggs
100 g/4 oz self-raising flour
2 teaspoons ground mixed spice

Grease the base and sides of a 20-cm/8-inch cake tin.

Cream 25 g/1 oz of the butter with 25 g/1 oz of the sugar until light and fluffy and spread over the base of the prepared tin. Drain the pineapple and halve the cherries. Arrange the pineapple, cherries and walnuts in a pattern on the base of the tin.

Cream the remaining butter and sugar until light and fluffy. Beat the eggs and add gradually to the creamed mixture. Sift the flour and spice over the top and fold in with a metal spoon. Add a little milk if the mixture is too stiff.

Spread the mixture over the pineapple and smooth the top. Cook in a moderately hot oven (190°C, 375°F, Gas Mark 5) for 30–40 minutes. Invert on to a plate and allow the syrup to run down the cake.

Serve hot with custard.

Variation
For a special treat serve with whipped cream flavoured with brandy or an orange liqueur.

Baked Apple Roly-poly

Approximate preparation time: 30 minutes
Cooking time: 40 minutes
Serves 6

275 g/10 oz self-raising flour
pinch of salt
150 g/5 oz shredded suet
450 g/1 lb cooking apples
75 g/3 oz demerara or soft brown sugar
2 teaspoons ground cinnamon
75 g/3 oz sultanas
milk and sugar to glaze

Sift the flour and salt into a bowl. Stir in enough cold water to make a soft, but not sticky dough. Roll out on a lightly floured surface to a 30×35-cm/12×14-inch rectangle. Trim the edges and cut a 5-cm/2-inch wide strip from the shorter side.

Peel, core and chop the apples and spread over the suet pastry to within 2.5 cm/1 inch of the edges. Mix the sugar, cinnamon and sultanas and sprinkle over the apple. Fold the pastry edges over the filling on both the long sides. Brush the sides and both ends with water and roll up from the shorter side like a Swiss roll. Seal the ends.

Place the roll, join underneath, on a piece of foil on a baking tray. Push up the sides of the foil to keep the roll in shape. Gather up the pastry trimmings and the cut strip and roll in two thin sausage shapes. Twist together and place down the centre of the roll. Brush all over with milk. Make five slits down each side of the roll to let steam escape.

Cook in a moderately hot oven (200°C, 400°F, Gas Mark 6) for about 40 minutes. Cover with foil if it browns too quickly.

Serve hot with custard.

Plum and Almond Whirls

Approximate preparation time: 20 minutes
Cooking time: 25 minutes
Serves 4–6

225 g/8 oz self-raising flour
$\frac{1}{2}$ teaspoon salt
100 g/4 oz shredded suet
150 ml/$\frac{1}{4}$ pint milk
175 g/6 oz plum jam
25 g/1 oz soft brown sugar
25 g/1 oz flaked almonds

Lightly grease a 25-cm/10-inch flan dish.

Sift the flour and salt into a bowl and mix in the suet. Stir in enough milk to make a soft dough. Roll out on a lightly floured surface to a 30-cm/12-inch square.

Spread the jam over the dough to within 2.5 cm/1 inch of the edges. Damp the edges of the dough and roll up. Cut into ten to twelve slices and arrange in the prepared dish. Cook in a moderately hot oven (200°C, 400°F, Gas Mark 6) for about 15 minutes. Sprinkle with the sugar and almonds then return to the oven for a further 10 minutes.

Serve hot.

Accompaniments
Serve with a fruit-flavoured yogurt or extra jam, heated and poured over.

Peach and Raspberry Pudding

Approximate preparation time: 20 minutes
Cooking time: 30–35 minutes
Serves 4–6

1 (396-g/14-oz) can peach halves
90 g/$3\frac{1}{2}$ oz butter
75 g/3 oz castor sugar
1 egg
150 g/5 oz self-raising flour
$\frac{1}{2}$ teaspoon vanilla essence
7 teaspoons raspberry jam

Grease a 1-litre/$1\frac{1}{2}$-pint pudding basin with 15 g/1 oz of the butter. Drain the peaches, reserving the juice. Arrange the peaches, cut side down, over the base of the prepared basin.

Cream the remaining butter with the sugar until light and fluffy. Beat the egg and add gradually to the creamed mixture. Sift the flour over the top and fold in with the vanilla essence using a metal spoon. Turn into the basin and cook in a moderate oven (180°C, 350°F, Gas Mark 4) for 30–35 minutes. Turn out and place a teaspoon of jam in the centre of each peach half.

Serve hot.

Accompaniments

Either serve with custard or cream or for a special occasion, make a banana sauce. Peel three large bananas and mash well. Put in a pan with the juice of 1 lemon and 25 g/1 oz brown sugar. Heat gently until the sugar dissolves then serve hot with the pudding.

Orange Loaf

Approximate preparation time: 25 minutes
Cooking time: 45 minutes
Serves 6–8

100 g/4 oz glacé cherries
50 g/2 oz angelica
100 g/4 oz unsalted butter
100 g/4 oz castor sugar
grated rind and juice of 1 small orange
2 eggs
50 g/2 oz fresh white breadcrumbs
75 g/3 oz self-raising flour
3 tablespoons marmalade
1 medium orange

Grease a 1.5-kg/1-lb loaf tin.

Roughly chop the cherries and angelica. Cream the butter and sugar until light and fluffy then add the orange rind. Beat the eggs and add gradually to the creamed mixture. Add the orange juice and chopped fruit. Sift the flour over the top, add the breadcrumbs and fold in with a metal spoon.

Coat the base and sides of the prepared tin with the marmalade; slice the orange and arrange over the base and sides. Turn the pudding mixture into the tin, spread evenly and stand in a roasting tin half-filled with water. Cook in a moderately hot oven (200°C, 400°F, Gas Mark 6) for about 45 minutes. Turn out and let the marmalade run down the sides.

Serve hot with custard or cream.

Variations

If you like a sharper flavour, use lemon instead of orange, using only 1 teaspoon of the rind. For a special occasion, flavour the cream with an orange liqueur or brandy.

Blackberry and Apple Sponge

Approximate preparation time: 25
minutes
Cooking time: 1 hour 10 minutes
Serves 5–6

675 g/1½ lb cooking apples
1 (284-g/10-oz) can blackberries
100 g/4 oz granulated sugar
100 g/4 oz butter
100 g/4 oz castor sugar
2 eggs
grated rind of 1 small orange
100 g/4 oz self-raising flour
icing sugar to decorate

Grease a 1.5-litre/2½-pint ovenproof dish.

Peel, core and quarter the apples, slice thinly and put in the prepared dish. Drain half the juice from the can of blackberries and add the remaining juice and fruit to the dish. Sprinkle the granulated sugar on top and mix lightly.

Cream the butter and castor sugar until fluffy. Beat the eggs and add gradually to the creamed mixture. Beat in the orange rind. Sift the flour over the top and fold in with a metal spoon. Spread over the fruit, covering it completely and smooth the top with a knife.

Cook in a moderate oven (180°C, 350°F, Gas Mark 4) for 1 hour 10 minutes. Sift a little icing sugar over the top and serve hot.

Rhubarb Cobbler

Approximate preparation time: 25
minutes
Cooking time: 20–25 minutes
Serves 6

900 g/2 lb rhubarb
75 g/3 oz castor sugar, plus 2
tablespoons
225 g/8 oz self-raising flour
pinch of salt
50 g/2 oz butter or margarine
150 ml/¼ pint milk
milk to glaze
castor sugar to sprinkle

Trim and chop the rhubarb. Put in a pan with 75 g/3 oz of the sugar and 2 tablespoons water. Cover and simmer for 5 minutes or until just tender. Turn into an ovenproof dish.

Sift the flour and salt into a bowl, cut the butter or margarine into pieces and rub in with the fingertips until the mixture resembles fine breadcrumbs. Stir in the remaining sugar. Make a well in the centre and add enough milk to make a soft dough. Roll out on a lightly floured surface to a 1-cm/½-inch thick round. Cut out 5-cm/2-inch rounds with a cutter. Arrange the rounds overlapping on top of the fruit. Brush the rounds with milk and sprinkle with sugar. Cook in a hot oven (220°C, 425°F, Gas Mark 7) for 10–15 minutes.

Serve at once.

Accompaniments
Orange marmalade sauce is good with rhubarb. Mix ½ teaspoon arrowroot with a little water. Make up to 150 ml/¼ pint with water. Bring to the boil and cook, stirring for 2 minutes. Stir in 3 tablespoons orange marmalade and 1 teaspoon orange juice. Serve hot with the cobbler.

Pear Pan Dowdy

Approximate preparation time: 25
minutes
Cooking time: 35 minutes
Serves 6

100 g/4 oz brown sugar
100 g/4 oz plain flour, plus an extra
2 teaspoons
pinch of salt
1 teaspoon cider vinegar
grated rind of 1 small lemon
pinch of ground cinnamon
pinch of grated nutmeg
25 g/1 oz butter
900 g/2 lb Conference pears
2 teaspoons baking powder
50 g/2 oz margarine
150 ml/¼ pint milk

Put the sugar in a saucepan with the 2
teaspoons flour and a pinch of salt. Mix the
vinegar with 150 ml/¼ pint water, then stir
into the pan. When smooth, bring to the
boil and simmer for 3 minutes, stirring
continuously.

Remove from the heat and stir in the
lemon rind, cinnamon, nutmeg and butter.

Peel and core the pears. Cut in slices and
arrange in an ovenproof dish, reserving a
few slices for a decoration. Pour the sauce
over the pears.

Sift the remaining flour with the baking
powder and a pinch of salt. Cut the margarine into pieces and rub into the flour with
the fingertips until the mixture resembles
fine breadcrumbs. Gradually stir in the milk,
beating until smooth. Spread over the pears
and cook in a moderately hot oven (200°C,
400°F, Gas Mark 6) for about 30 minutes.
Decorate with the reserved pear slices.

Variations
Apples can be used instead of pears. Raspberry jam, heated, makes a good sauce.

Cherry Clafoutie

Approximate preparation time: 10
minutes
Cooking time: 30–35 minutes
Serves 6

450 g/1 lb black cherries
4 eggs
100 g/4 oz plain flour
3 tablespoons clear honey
600 ml/1 pint milk, warmed
25 g/1 oz butter
whipped cream to serve

Grease a shallow ovenproof dish.

Stone the cherries and remove the stalks.
Beat the eggs and gradually add the flour,
honey and milk. Add the cherries to the
batter and pour into the prepared dish. Cook
in a hot oven (220°C, 425°F, Gas Mark 7)
for 30–35 minutes.

Serve at once with whipped cream.

Variation
Peaches make a good sauce for this dish.
Peel 450 g/1 lb peaches and remove the
stones. Purée the fruit and place in a
saucepan with a little sugar and 2 tablespoons brandy. Heat gently without boiling
and serve with the clafoutie.

Apple and Almond Meringue

Approximate preparation time: 25
minutes
Cooking time: 20 minutes
Serves 4–6

900 g/2 lb cooking apples
225 g/8 oz castor sugar
50 g/2 oz ground almonds
½ teaspoon almond essence
50 g/2 oz sultanas
2 egg whites
flaked almonds, toasted

Peel, core and thinly slice the apples. Place in a saucepan with half the sugar and 3 tablespoons water. Heat to dissolve the sugar then cover and cook gently for 10 minutes. Purée the apple and add the ground almonds, almond essence and sultanas. Turn into an ovenproof dish.

Whisk the egg whites until stiff and standing in peaks. Whisk in half the remaining sugar and fold in the rest with a metal spoon. Fit a piping bag with a medium star nozzle and fill the bag with the meringue. Pipe the meringue over the apple in rosettes. Cook in a moderately hot oven (200°C, 400°F, Gas Mark 6) for 10 minutes or until golden. Decorate with the almonds.

Serve hot or cold.

Accompaniments
Serve with cream whipped with raspberry liqueur or chocolate liqueur mixed with brandy.

Fig and Apple Pudding

Approximate preparation time: 20
minutes
Cooking time: 35 minutes
Serves 6

20 dried figs
2 medium cooking apples
100 g/4 oz plain flour
225 g/8 oz brown sugar
50 g/2 oz butter
40 g/1½ oz walnuts
1 small red-skinned apple

Place the figs in a small basin. Pour in boiling water to cover and leave for 3 minutes. Drain and cut out the stems. Chop the flesh, leaving four whole.

Peel, core and slice the apples, mix with the figs and put in an ovenproof dish. Mix the flour with the sugar and rub in the butter until the mixture resembles fine breadcrumbs. Chop the walnuts and add all but 15 g/½ oz to the flour. Sprinkle over the apples and figs.

Cook in a moderately hot oven (190°C, 375°F, Gas Mark 5) for about 35 minutes.

Core the apple and slice thinly. Use with the whole figs and remaining walnuts to decorate the pudding.

Serve hot with custard or cream.

Raspberry Crumble

Approximate preparation time: 15
minutes
Cooking time: 40–45 minutes
Serves 4–6

1 (439-g/15½-oz) can raspberries
1 tablespoon arrowroot
175 g/6 oz plain flour
pinch of salt
75 g/3 oz butter
40 g/1½ oz castor sugar
150 ml/¼ pint double cream

Drain the juice from the raspberries and mix it with the arrowroot. Pour into a small saucepan and bring to the boil, stirring continuously. Leave to cool then stir in the raspberries. Pour into a 1.25-litre/2-pint pie dish.

Sift the flour and salt into a bowl. Cut the butter into pieces and rub in with the fingertips until the mixture resembles coarse breadcrumbs. Stir in the sugar then use the mixture to cover the raspberries. Cook in a hot oven (220°C, 425°F, Gas Mark 7) for about 30 minutes.

Serve hot or cold with cream.

Apricot and Apple Charlotte

Approximate preparation time: 15
minutes
Cooking time: 1 hour
Serves 4–6

7 thick slices from a large white
loaf
50 g/2 oz butter
1 large cooking apple
1 (425-g/15-oz) can apricot pie
filling or apricots
50 g/2 oz soft brown sugar
25 g/1 oz flaked almonds
¼ teaspoon ground cinnamon

Cut the crusts from the bread and use two slices to make breadcrumbs. Use all but 15 g/1½ oz of the butter to spread over the remaining slices. Use the slices to line a 1.25-litre/2-pint ovenproof dish, buttered sides against the dish.

Peel, core and chop the apple and mix with the pie filling. (If using canned apricots, purée them first). Spoon into the lined dish.

Mix the breadcrumbs with the sugar, almonds and cinnamon and sprinkle over the top. Dot the remaining butter over the dish. Cook in a moderate oven (180°C, 350°F, Gas Mark 4) for about 1 hour.

Accompaniment
Serve with brandy butter made by creaming together 75 g/3 oz butter with 50 g/2 oz light soft brown sugar, 1 teaspoon grated orange rind and brandy to taste.

Baked Pear Charlotte

Approximate preparation time: 25 minutes
Cooking time: 45 minutes to 1 hour
Serves 5–6

15 g/$\frac{1}{2}$ oz butter
150 g/5 oz brown sugar
6 slices buttered bread
900 g/2 lb firm pears
grated rind and strained juice of 1 small lemon

Grease a 1.25-litre/2-pint pudding basin or charlotte mould with the butter. Sprinkle over 25 g/1 oz of the sugar. Cut the crusts from the buttered bread and use most of the slices to line the basin.

Peel, core and slice the pears and layer them in the basin with the sugar, lemon rind and juice. Cover the pudding with the remaining slices. Cover with greased foil and cook in a moderate oven (180°C, 350°F, Gas Mark 4) for about 45 minutes.

Turn out and serve hot with cream.

Accompaniment

Try a sabayon sauce with the charlotte. Beat 3 egg yolks with 75 g/3 oz sugar until light and add a glass of white wine. Stand in a pan of hot water and bring to the boil, whisking all the time. Remove from the heat and whisk for 2 minutes. Serve the thick sauce at once while hot.

Bread and Butter Pudding

Approximate preparation time: 15 minutes (plus standing time)
Cooking time: 30–35 minutes
Serves 4

5 large slices buttered bread
50 g/2 oz mixed dried fruit
50 g/2 oz demerara sugar
2 eggs
450 ml/$\frac{3}{4}$ pint milk
$\frac{1}{4}$ teaspoon ground mixed spice or grated nutmeg

Grease a 1.25-litre/2-pint pie dish.

Cut the crusts from the bread and cut each slice into quarters. Put a layer of bread into the prepared dish. Sprinkle with some dried fruit and sugar. Continue these layers until the ingredients are used up.

Lightly beat the eggs and add the milk and spice or nutmeg. Pour over the pudding and leave for 15 minutes.

Cook in a moderate oven (180°C, 350°F, Gas Mark 4) for 30–35 minutes.

Serve immediately.

Accompaniments

Serve with cream whipped with a little orange rind, ice cream or honey-flavoured yogurt.

If liked the milk can be flavoured with a few drops of vanilla or almond essence.

Bread Pudding

Approximate preparation time: 15 minutes (plus standing time)
Cooking time: 2–2¼ hours
Serves 6

450 g/1 lb stale white bread
75 g/3 oz shredded suet
50 g/2 oz chopped mixed peel
75 g/3 oz currants
75 g/3 oz sultanas
1 teaspoon ground mixed spice
pinch of grated nutmeg
75 g/3 oz castor sugar
1 egg
4 tablespoons milk
castor sugar to sprinkle

Grease a deep 20-cm/8-inch square cake tin.

Break the bread into small pieces and place in a bowl. Cover with cold water and stand for 40 minutes. Squeeze the bread until very dry and transfer to a clean bowl.

Mix the suet, peel, currants, sultanas, spice, nutmeg and sugar into the bread. Beat in the egg and milk.

Turn into the prepared tin and smooth the top. Cook in a moderately hot oven (190°C, 375°F, Gas Mark 5) for 2–2¼ hours. Dredge with sugar.

Serve hot or cold.

Lemon Baked Apples

Approximate preparation time: 10 minutes
Cooking time: 45 minutes–1 hour
Serves 5

5 medium cooking apples
75 g/3 oz mixed dried fruit
50 g/2 oz light soft brown sugar
finely grated rind and juice of 1 small lemon
15 g/½ oz butter

Core the apples and make a scored mark through the skin around each apple. Stand the apples in an ovenproof dish and stuff the core cavities with the dried fruit. Mix the sugar with the lemon rind and juice and 2 tablespoons of water and pour over the apples. Dot with the butter, cover with a lid or foil and cook in a moderately hot oven (200°C, 400°F, Gas Mark 6) for about 50 minutes.

Variations
Stuff the apples with home-made mincemeat, a mixture of honey and chopped dates or orange marmalade.

Accompaniment
Serve with rum butter made as follows. Beat 50 g/2 oz butter with 50 g/2 oz brown sugar and lemon juice. Beat in rum to taste.

Rice Pudding

Approximate preparation time: 5 minutes
Cooking time: 2 hours
Serves 4

3 tablespoons short-grain rice
2 tablespoons castor sugar
600 ml/1 pint milk
25 g/1 oz butter
little grated nutmeg

Grease a 1-litre/1½-pint ovenproof dish.

Rinse the rice and put in the prepared dish with the sugar. Pour on the milk, dot with butter and sprinkle with nutmeg. Cook in a cool oven (150°C, 300°F, Gas Mark 2) for about 2 hours, stirring after 30 minutes.

Serve hot or cold.

Accompaniments
Serve with jam or syrup sauce or with fresh or canned fruit such as apricots or raspberries.

Spiced Fruit Semolina

Approximate preparation time: 25 minutes
Cooking time: 1 hour
Serves 4–6

600 ml/1 pint milk
40 g/1½ oz semolina
2 eggs, separated
100 g/4 oz castor sugar
1 teaspoon ground mixed spice
grated rind of ½ small lemon, plus a thin strip of lemon peel
50 g/2 oz sultanas
225 g/8 oz granulated sugar
450 g/1 lb dessert apples
angelica to decorate

Grease a 1.25-litre/2-pint ovenproof dish.

Heat the milk in a saucepan, sprinkle over the semolina and bring to the boil. Cook for about 10 minutes, stirring continuously.

Beat the egg yolks. Remove the pan from the heat and stir in half the sugar with the spice, grated rind and sultanas. Stir 2 tablespoons of the hot semolina into the egg yolks and mix back into the pudding. Turn into the prepared dish and cook in a moderate oven (180°C, 350°F, Gas Mark 4) for about 20 minutes.

Dissolve the granulated sugar in 300 ml/½ pint water then boil for 5 minutes. Add the lemon peel.

Peel, core and slice the apples then poach in the syrup for about 10 minutes. Drain.

Whisk the egg whites until stiff and standing in peaks. Whisk in the remaining sugar. Reduce the oven to cool (150°C, 300°F, Gas Mark 2). Spread the apple over the cooked pudding. Spread or pipe the meringue over the apple and cook for 10 minutes to brown the meringue. Decorate with pieces of angelica.

Serve hot or cold.

Noodles Jubilee

Approximate preparation time: 5 minutes
Cooking time: 15 minutes
Serves 4

225 g/8 oz egg noodles
1 (425-g/15-oz) can black cherries
2 teaspoons cornflour
1 tablespoon brandy
2 tablespoons clear honey
50 g/2 oz almonds, very finely chopped

Cook the noodles in boiling water until tender, about 10 minutes.

Meanwhile, drain the cherries and pour the juice into a saucepan. Bring to the boil. Mix the cornflour to a paste with 2 tablespoons cold water. Stir into the cherry juice and cook, stirring until thick and smooth. Stir in the brandy and cherries and heat through gently.

Drain the cooked noodles and mix with the honey and cherries in the sauce. Heat gently and serve sprinkled with the almonds.

Accompaniments
Serve with whipped cream mixed with Kirsch, brandy or a cherry-flavoured liqueur. Natural yogurt makes a good sharp contrast in flavour.

Cottage Cheese Pancakes

Approximate preparation time: 20 minutes
Cooking time: 15–20 minutes
Serves 4–6

100 g/4 oz plain flour
pinch of salt
1 egg
300 ml/$\frac{1}{2}$ pint milk
lard or oil for frying
225 g/8 oz cottage cheese
75 g/3 oz sultanas
50 g/2 oz castor sugar
lemon wedges

Sift the flour with the salt. Make a well in the centre and break the egg into it. Add half the milk and gradually mix in the flour, drawing it from the edges with a wooden spoon. Add the remaining milk and beat until smooth.

Heat a knob of lard or a little oil in a frying pan. When a blue haze appears over the pan pour in a little batter and tilt the pan to cover the base with batter. Cook until the underside is brown. Toss or flip with a palette knife and cook the other side. Keep the cooked pancakes hot while repeating with the rest of the mixture.

Mix the cottage cheese, sultanas and half the castor sugar together. Use to fill the pancakes, folding them into envelope shapes.

Serve hot sprinkled with the remaining sugar with the lemon wedges.

Pancakes with Liqueur Sauce

Approximate preparation time: 15 minutes
Cooking time: 10–15 minutes
Serves 4–6

100 g/4 oz plain flour
pinch of salt
1 egg
300 ml/$\frac{1}{2}$ pint milk
lard or oil for frying
1 (500-ml/32.5-fl oz) block vanilla ice cream
175 g/6 oz chunky orange marmalade
2 tablespoons Cointreau or Grand Marnier

Sift the flour and salt into a bowl. Make a well in the centre and break in the egg. Add half the milk and gradually draw in the flour from the edges, using a wooden spoon. Beat until smooth then add the remaining milk.

Heat a knob of lard or a little oil in a frying pan. When a haze appears over the pan, pour in a little batter and tilt the pan to cover the base with batter. When the underside is golden, toss or flip over with a palette knife and cook the other side. Keep cooked pancakes hot while you repeat with the remaining batter.

Fill each pancake with a slice of ice cream and roll up. Heat the marmalade and liqueur together and spoon over the pancakes.

Serve immediately.

Variations
Use a chocolate sauce instead of a liqueur one. Melt 50 g/2 oz plain chocolate with 15 g/1$\frac{1}{2}$ oz butter and 1$\frac{1}{2}$ tablespoons milk. Serve hot. If liked simply serve the pancakes with heated jam.

COLD DESSERTS

Lemon Ice

Approximate preparation time: 20
minutes (plus standing time)
Cooking time: 10 minutes
Serves 6

**225 g/8 oz granulated sugar
grated rind and juice of 2 large
lemons**

Dissolve the sugar in 300 ml/$\frac{1}{2}$ pint water in a saucepan. Bring to the boil and boil for 1 minute. Leave to cool. Mix the lemon rind with the syrup, infuse for 2 hours then strain. Stir the juice into the syrup. Pour into a shallow freezer tray, cover with foil and freeze overnight. Remove to the refrigerator for 15 minutes before serving.

Serve in frosted glasses – dip the rims of glasses in egg white, then in castor sugar. Leave to dry before using the glasses.

Making Ice Cream

Ice cream is as easy to make as an egg custard, and the results are truly delicious. Don't be put off if you don't have a freezer; you can make ice cream in the ice-box of an ordinary refrigerator.

Checkpoints: if you are using a refrigerator, make sure the container you choose will fit into the ice-making compartment – try it for size before you start. Turn the refrigerator to its coldest setting 1 hour before you start to make the ice cream – the faster it freezes, the better the texture will be.

Preventing ice crystals: freeze the mixture for an hour or until the mixture is set round the edges. Take out of the container and whisk thoroughly. Put back in the container; cover with foil and leave until hard-frozen. Remember to turn the refrigerator back to its normal setting once ice cream is ready. Ice creams made in bombe moulds are not usually beaten halfway through freezing.

Serving the ice cream: let it stand in the ordinary part of the refrigerator for 15 minutes before serving – if it is too frozen the flavour won't come through.

Simple basic recipe: bring 300 ml/$\frac{1}{2}$ pint milk and 75 g/3 oz castor sugar almost to boiling point. Beat 1 egg with 2 egg yolks. Pour on the hot milk. Mix well and flavour with vanilla essence, to taste. Strain the mixture into a clean pan. Keep over a very low heat and stir all the time until the mixture is thick enough to coat the back of a wooden spoon. Put in a basin and leave to cool. Lightly whip 300 ml/$\frac{1}{2}$ pint double cream and fold into the mixture; now it's ready for freezing.

Looking good: ice cream looks extra attractive served in scoops, but you can get almost the same effect with a tablespoon, if you dip it in warm water before use. Glass dishes, or large wine glasses, show off the ice cream really well and in a silver goblet the ice cream looks superb. Fan biscuits add the finishing touch.

Apricot Ice Cream

Approximate preparation time: 15
minutes (plus standing time)
Cooking time: 7 minutes
Serves 2

1 (227 g/18 oz) can apricot halves
300 ml/$\frac{1}{2}$ pint single cream
2 large eggs
3 tablespoons granulated sugar
2 fan wafers
15 g/$\frac{1}{2}$ oz blanched almonds, toasted

Turn the refrigerator to its coldest setting 1
hour before starting the ice cream. Drain the
apricots then chop very finely.

Put the cream in the pan with the eggs
and sugar. Beat well and cook over a low
heat, stirring continuously until the mixture
will coat the back of a spoon. Do not boil.

Pour the mixture into a bowl and cool.
Fold in the fruit and pour into a freezing tray.

Freeze for 1 hour or until it has frozen
1 cm/$\frac{1}{2}$ inch in from the edges. Turn into a
mixing bowl and whisk until smooth.
Return to the freezing tray, cover and freeze
for 4–5 hours. Move to the refrigerator 15
minutes before serving.

Serve in scoops sprinkled with the toasted almonds.

Variations
Use other canned fruit, or flavour the ice
cream with 2 teaspoons instant coffee dissolved in 1 tablespoon boiling water. Add
before folding in the fruit then proceed as
above.

Rum Ice Cream

Approximate preparation time: 20
minutes (plus standing time)
Cooking time: 10 minutes
Serves 4

3 large eggs
300 ml/$\frac{1}{2}$ pint milk
75 g/3 oz castor sugar
2 tablespoons cocoa powder
150 ml/$\frac{1}{4}$ pint double cream
4 tablespoons single cream
rum essence to taste
cream and nuts for decoration

Turn the refrigerator to its lowest setting
before you start the ice cream.

Separate 1 egg. Mix the yolk with the milk
and the remaining whole eggs. Stir in the
sugar and cocoa. Strain the mixture into the
top of a double saucepan and cook, stirring
gently until slightly thickened. Cool.

Whisk the egg white until stiff. Whip the
double and single cream together. Fold the
egg white and cream into the cooled mixture. Add rum essence to taste then pour
into a freezing container. Freeze for 1 hour,
transfer to a bowl and whisk well. Return to
the freezing tray, cover with foil and freeze
for 4–5 hours.

Remove to the refrigerator 15 minutes
before serving. Decorate with the cream and
nuts.

Chocolate Ice Cream

Approximate preparation time: 20
minutes (plus standing time)
Cooking time: 10 minutes
Serves 4

3 large eggs
300 ml / $\frac{1}{2}$ pint milk
75 g / 3 oz castor sugar
2 tablespoons cocoa powder
150 ml / $\frac{1}{4}$ pint double cream
4 tablespoons single cream
extra whipped cream and shredded
orange rind for decoration

Turn the refrigerator to its lowest setting before making the ice cream.

Separate one egg. Beat the yolk with the remaining whole eggs. Mix the milk with the sugar and cocoa, then strain and mix with the eggs. Pour into the top of a double saucepan and cook, stirring, until it thickens a little. Leave to cool.

Whisk the egg white until stiff. Whip the double and single cream together and fold into the cooled mixture with the egg whites. Turn into a freezing container and freeze for 1 hour. Turn into a bowl and whisk until smooth. Return to the freezing tray, cover with foil and freeze for 4–5 hours.

Move to the refrigerator 15 minutes before serving.

Party Bombe

Approximate preparation time: 25
minutes (plus standing time)
Cooking time: 10 minutes
Serves 6

3 egg yolks
300 ml / $\frac{1}{2}$ pint milk
300 ml / $\frac{1}{2}$ pint single cream
100 g / 4 oz icing sugar
few drops vanilla essence
150 ml / $\frac{1}{4}$ pint double cream
1 tablespoon strawberry milk-shake
syrup
175 g / 6 oz strawberries

This bombe needs to be made using a freezer, as the mould will not fit into an ice-box compartment.

Whisk the egg yolks and milk together thoroughly. Mix in the single cream, sift the icing sugar on top and stir in with the vanilla essence. Pour into the top of a double saucepan and cook, stirring until the mixture coats the back of a spoon. Pour into a 1-litre / 1$\frac{1}{2}$-pint bombe mould. Cover with foil and freeze for 6 hours. Dip the mould quickly in hot water and unmould. Turn on to a serving plate. Whip the double cream and fold in the milk-shake syrup. Decorate the mould with the cream and strawberries.

Serve at once.

Variation
Give the bombe a coffee flavour by adding 2 teaspoons instant coffee dissolved in 1 tablespoon boiling water. Omit the vanilla. Flavour the cream with brandy and decorate with grated chocolate.

Pineapple Bombe

Approximate preparation time: 25
minutes (plus standing time)
Cooking time: 10 minutes
Serves 4

3 egg yolks
300 ml/$\frac{1}{2}$ pint milk
300 ml/$\frac{1}{2}$ pint single cream
100 g/4 oz icing sugar
few drops vanilla essence
25 g/1 oz raisins, chopped
25 g/1 oz glacé pineapple
pineapple rings and canned cherries
for decoration

You need a freezer to make this dessert; the
mould would not fit in the ice-box compartment of an ordinary refrigerator.

Whisk together the egg yolks and milk in
the top of a double saucepan until well
mixed. Stir in the cream, sift the icing sugar
on top and mix in with the vanilla essence.
Cook, stirring in the double saucepan until
the mixture thickens. Cool a little then stir in
the raisins and pineapple.

Pour into a 1-litre/1$\frac{1}{2}$-pint bombe mould
and freeze for 6 hours. Dip quickly in hot
water to turn it out. Arrange the pineapple
rings and cherries around the base. If using a
fresh pineapple, use the leaves as an attractive decoration.

Serve immediately.

Meringue Glory

Approximate preparation time: 10
minutes
Serves 3–4

2 tablespoons gin
375 g/12 oz ripe raspberries
25 g/1 oz castor sugar
1 (227-g/8-oz) can peach slices
6 small meringue shells
1 (500-ml/17.6-fl oz) block vanilla ice
cream

Sprinkle the gin over the raspberries and stir
in the sugar. Put the raspberries, peach
slices and meringue shells in a serving bowl.
Cut the ice cream into chunks and add to the
bowl.

Serve at once.

Variations
Sandwich the meringues together in pairs
with whipped cream before adding to the
dish, or try different ice cream flavours such
as raspberry ripple or peach melba.

Accompaniments
Try one of the following sauces with the
dish. Heat raspberry jam with a little water,
or heat peach or apricot jam with water and
chopped walnuts. Remember to prepare the
sauce before getting the ice cream out of the
freezer.

Banana Boat

Approximate preparation time: 10
minutes
Serves 1

4 tablespoons double cream
25 g/1 oz unsalted peanuts
3 scoops vanilla or strawberry ice
cream
1 large banana
juice of 1 small orange
1 tablespoon pineapple milk-shake
syrup
1 glacé cherry and a few chocolate
curls for decoration

Whisk the cream until thick enough to pipe. Put half the nuts in a boat-shaped dish and chop the rest.

Put the ice cream in the dish. Peel and slice the banana and add to the dish. Mix the orange juice and milk shake syrup and brush over the banana. This adds a good flavour and prevents discoloration.

Sprinkle half the chopped nuts over the bananas and the rest over the ice cream. Top the dish with a swirl of whipped cream. Decorate with the cherry and chocolate curls and serve at once.

Accompaniments
To make the dessert even more sumptuous, serve with a jam or chocolate sauce.

Banana Delicious

Approximate preparation time: 15
minutes
Serves 1–2

4 scoops vanilla ice cream
1 medium banana
juice of 1 small lemon
175 g/6 oz ripe redcurrants
2–3 tablespoons redcurrant jelly
1 tablespoon chocolate sauce
biscuits for decoration

Arrange the scoops of ice cream on an oblong dish. Peel and slice the banana and toss in the lemon juice to prevent discoloration. Place the banana on the ice cream dish. Add the redcurrants, redcurrant-jelly and chocolate sauce. Decorate with the biscuits and serve immediately.

Variations
If liked replace the redcurrants with blackcurrants. Unless these are very sweet, you will need to cook them lightly with a little sugar. Allow to cool and use with an orange sauce instead of chocolate. Grate the rind and squeeze the juice from an orange and make up to $150 \, ml/\frac{1}{4}$ pint with water. Sweeten to taste. Stir 1 teaspoon cornflour with a little of the liquid. Bring the rest to the boil and stir into the cornflour. Return to the pan and bring to the boil stirring. Leave until cold before using with the ice cream.

Strawberry Marinade

Approximate preparation time: 10
minutes (plus standing time)
Serves 4

450 g/1 lb strawberries
juice of 1 medium orange
2 tablespoons brandy or strawberry
liqueur
1 (500-ml/17.6-fl oz) block vanilla
ice cream straight from the freezer

Put the strawberries in a non-metal dish. Mix the orange juice with the brandy or liqueur and sprinkle over the strawberries. Leave for up to 3 hours – any longer and the straw-berries may become soggy.

Cut the ice cream into chunks and pile into serving dishes. Serve the strawberries in separate dishes and let people help them-selves to the ice cream. Serve at once.

Variations

Try different ice cream flavours such as chocolate, mint or chocolate chip. If liked, toast some flaked almonds and sprinkle over the dessert just before serving; sprinkle with chocolate curls.

Giant Sundae

Approximate preparation time: 10
minutes
Cooking time: 20 minutes
Serve 2–4

450 g/1 lb redcurrants
50 g/2 oz castor sugar
wineglass of port
1 teaspoon arrowroot or cornflour
1 (500-ml/17.6-fl oz) block vanilla
ice cream straight from the freezer

Put the redcurrants in a pan with the sugar and 5 tablespoons water. Simmer, covered, for 15 minutes or until tender. If the mixture is not sweet enough, add extra sugar. Stir in the port.

Mix the arrowroot or cornflour with a little water and stir into the redcurrants. Heat, stirring until the mixture thickens. Leave to cool completely.

Scoop the ice cream into a large serving dish. Spoon the redcurrants on top and serve at once.

Variations

The same topping method can be used with blackcurrants or gooseberries and, if liked, sprinkle with toasted chopped almonds and hazelnuts and add a swirl of whipped cream.

Fresh Peach Sundae

Approximate preparation time: 15
minutes
Serves 1

**1 very large ripe peach
4 tablespoons sweet white wine or
Strega liqueur
1–2 tablespoons double cream
2–3 scoops vanilla or strawberry ice
cream
finger biscuit for serving**

Peel the peach using a stainless steel knife, or blanch quickly and remove the skin with your fingers. Remove the stone and slice the flesh neatly, reserving any juices.

Stir the peaches, juice and wine or Strega together, taking care not to break the slices up. Put half the mixture in to a large glass. Whip the cream lightly and spread on top. Add the remaining peach and liquid. Top with the ice cream and decorate with the biscuit.

Serve at once.

Accompaniment

Serve with a Melba sauce. Mix 1 tablespoon redcurrant jelly with 2 teaspoons castor sugar and a purée made from 100 g/4 oz raspberries. Thicken with arrowroot, strain and leave to cool. Serve over the sundae.

Grape Fancy

Approximate preparation time: 7 minutes
Serves 1

**175 g/6 oz green grapes
2 teaspoons clear honey
2 scoops vanilla ice cream
4 tablespoons double cream or
made-up dessert topping
15 g/$\frac{1}{2}$ oz toasted chopped almonds
or a few unsalted peanuts, finely
chopped.**

If you prefer grapes without skins, peel them before removing the ice cream from the freezer. Reserve a few grapes for decoration. Put the grapes in a dish and spoon the honey on top. Add the ice cream and a swirl of cream or dessert topping. Sprinkle with the nuts.

Serve at once.

Accompaniment

Serve with a mocha sauce. Put 25 g/1 oz plain chocolate in the top of a double saucepan with 7 g/$\frac{1}{4}$ oz butter and 2 teaspoons strong black coffee. Melt the chocolate and cool a little. Spoon over the ice cream.

Grape facts

Most of the grapes we eat in this country are imported, but some very fine grapes are grown in Britain, under glass. When choosing grapes, look for ones with a distinct bloom on the skin. Avoid any that show traces of mould near the stem and any that are shrivelled or have broken skins.

Muscat grapes are especially good with their slightly perfumed flavour and golden colour.

Amongst the black grapes, Alicante are of the better known varieties; they have purple skins and are extra juicy.

Allow plenty of time if you want to peel grapes – it's a very fiddly job. The pips can be removed with a hair-pin.

Lemony Treats

Approximate preparation time: 15
minutes (plus standing time)
Cooking time: 5 minutes
Serves 3

1 packet lemon pie-filling
300 ml/$\frac{1}{2}$ pint boiling water
1 egg yolk
few cooked blackcurrants
275 g/10 oz strawberries
4 scoops strawberry ice cream
150 ml/$\frac{1}{4}$ pint double cream or
made-up dessert topping

Following the packet instructions to make up the pie filling using the egg yolk. Cover with cling film and leave to cool. Chill for up to 4 hours.

Divide the blackcurrants between three wine glasses. Top with the pie filling and then some of the strawberries and the ice cream. Whip the cream and add to the sundae. Decorate with the remaining strawberries.

Serve at once.

Variations
Make lemon blancmange instead of pie filling and chill well. If strawberries are scarce, use unpeeled, red skinned apples, cored and sliced. Toss in lemon or orange juice and mix with orange segments.

Chocolate Spoon Sweet

Approximate preparation time: 10
minutes
Serves 1

2 scoops soft variety vanilla ice
cream
2 tablespoons chocolate sauce
15 g/$\frac{1}{2}$ oz chopped almonds or
chopped unsalted peanuts

Let the ice cream stand at room temperature for 5 minutes then stir in the chocolate sauce, just a little – but don't mix in. Try for an attractive marbled effect. Put the mixture in a large wine glass. Sprinkle the nuts on top and serve at once.

Variations
It is easiest to use bought chocolate sauce, but if you like, make your own. Melt 25 g/1 oz bitter chocolate and 175 g/6 oz butter with 2 teaspoons creamy milk in the top of a double saucepan. Stir well, cool, then mix with the ice cream as above. This may harden on contact with the ice cream, but it is still delicious.

For a richer flavour, use the soft variety rum and raisin flavour. Top with double cream.

Rich Chocolate Sundae

Approximate preparation time: 15
minutes
Serves 1

150 ml/$\frac{1}{4}$ pint double cream
2 teaspoons drinking chocolate
1 large scoop chocolate ice cream
chocolate vermicelli or grated
chocolate
1 biscuit and cocktail cherry for
decoration

Put half the cream in a small basin and whisk in the drinking chocolate until very well blended. Put this in a serving glass. Lightly whip the rest of the cream and spoon on top.

Now add the ice cream and sprinkle the chocolate vermicelli or grated chocolate on top. Decorate with the biscuit and cherry and serve immediately.

Variation
If liked, replace the cream with made up dessert topping. Chill before using.

Accompaniment
Serve with a coffee sauce. Dissolve 50 g/ 2 oz sugar in 2 tablespoons water. Boil until a rich golden colour. Mix in 4 tablespoons strong black coffee. Boil for 2 minutes, stirring. Allow to cool then pour over the ice cream.

Chocolate Liqueur Sweet

Approximate preparation time: 15
minutes (plus standing time)
Serves 4

1 layer chocolate sponge cake
3 tablespoons Tia Maria or crème
de cacao
2 individual frozen vanilla mousses
few chocolate sweets
12 whole almonds, halved and
toasted

Scoop out a little of the cake to make a shallow indent in the centre. Soak the cake in the chosen liqueur and chill in the refrigerator. Allow the mousses to thaw slightly.

Beat the mousse with a fork until fluffy and pile it on to the centre of the cake. Decorate with chocolate sweets and toasted almonds.

Serve immediately.

Variations
Try different flavours of bought or home-made mousse. Try coffee cake with raspberry mousse. For a change, decorate with piped cream and glacé or maraschino cherries.

Redcurrant Surprise

Approximate preparation time: 10
minutes (plus standing time)
Serves 1

3 tablespoons natural yogurt
175 g/6 oz ripe redcurrants
4 tablespoons double cream
1 teaspoon instant coffee powder
or very finely ground coffee beans
1 individual frozen chocolate
mousse

Put the yogurt in a large glass and put most of the redcurrants on top. Mix the cream with the coffee and whip until very thick. Add to the glass, then put in refrigerator to chill for 4 hours.

At the same time, put the mousse in the refrigerator to thaw a little.

Scoop out the mousse and arrange on top of the cream. Decorate the edge of the glass with a bunch of redcurrants. Serve at once.

Variations
Other raw seasonal fruit can replace the redcurrants, but they must be ripe enough and sweet enough to eat just as they are. Instead of using a bought mousse you could make up some custard – make it really thick – stir in a tablespoon of cream and chill thoroughly before using.

Top the custard with a little grated chocolate.

Orange Chiller

Approximate preparation time: 15
minutes (plus standing time)
Serves 1

4 tablespoons evaporated milk,
chilled overnight
1 teaspoon grated orange rind
1 tablespoon rum
$\frac{1}{2}$ (298-g/10$\frac{1}{2}$-oz) can mandarin
oranges
1 individual frozen vanilla mousse

The evaporated milk must be chilled overnight in the refrigerator or it will be impossible to whip.

Whip the chilled milk until it is very stiff and mix in the orange rind and rum. Drain the oranges, and spoon, with the whipped milk, into a serving glass. Add the vanilla mousse and chill for 4 hours in the bottom part of the refrigerator.

Variations
For a sharper flavour, leave out the rum and use lemon juice instead. Experiment with different flavours of bought mousse – chocolate goes especially well with orange. If you are serving this to children, add some chocolate orange segments or a row of chocolate buttons just before serving.

Greek Sundae

Approximate preparation time: 15
minutes (plus standing time)
Serves 1

$\frac{1}{2}$ slice of watermelon
grated rind and juice of 1 small
orange
4 tablespoons natural yogurt,
chilled
3 tablespoons double cream

Peel the watermelon and cut into small
chunks. Sprinkle the orange juice over the
melon and leave to stand for 2 hours in the
refrigerator. Mix the yogurt with 1 teaspoon
of the orange rind and most of the cream.

Spoon the yogurt mixture into a wine
glass, top with the melon and then add a
swirl of cream.

Serve at once.

Melon notes

Watermelon: *has a glossy dark skin
and bright-pink flesh with black
seeds. The largest melon, it is often
sold in slices.*
Charentais: *a small round melon,
yellow. Inside the flesh is orange-
yellow with a slightly scented flavour.*
Honeydew: *shaped like a rugby ball,
the skin can be green, yellow or white;
inside it's pale green and sweet.*
Cantaloupe: *a rough skin, green or
yellow. Inside it's orange-yellow with
a delicious scent.*
Ogen: *a small melon, very sweet and
juicy. It has yellow to orange skin
marked with faint greenish stripes. It is
named after the kibbutz in Israel where
it was first developed and is very
popular.*

Cranberry and Orange Cups

Approximate preparation time: 20
minutes (plus standing time)
Serves 4

4 good tablespoons cranberry jelly
$\frac{1}{2}$ packet orange jelly
150 ml/$\frac{1}{4}$ pint double cream
whisky to taste

Divide the cranberry jelly between four wine
glasses. Make up the jelly, using half the
amount of water suggested on the packet.
When it is beginning to set, spoon on top of
the cranberry jelly and leave to set in the
refrigerator.

Whip the cream and flavour it with the
whisky, mixing it in a drop at a time. Spoon
on top of the set jelly and serve at once, or
keep in the refrigerator for up to 5 hours
before serving.

Variations

When fresh cranberries are in the shops, use
these instead of cranberry jelly. Stew the
fresh cranberries with sugar to taste and a
little water for 5 minutes, or until tender. Mix
1 teaspoon cornflour with a little water. Stir
into the cranberries and bring to the boil,
stirring until thick. Leave to cool. Add the
cream and decorate with segments of
orange.

Melon Whip

Approximate preparation time: 15
minutes (plus standing time)
Serves 2

**1 small honeydew melon
1 (142-ml/5-fl oz) carton lemon
yogurt
150 ml/$\frac{1}{4}$ pint double cream
cherries and blackcurrants for
decoration
1 small milk chocolate flake bar**

Cut the melon in half and scoop out all the seeds. Cut the melon flesh into chunks and mix with the yogurt. Divide between two large glasses and chill for 4 hours.

Top the chilled yogurt mixture with some of the cherries and blackcurrants. Whip the cream until thick and pipe over the top. Serve at once – topped with the remaining cherries, blackcurrants and the milk chocolate flake bar.

Variations

If you like a sharp-tasting dessert use plain yogurt instead of lemon. If you like your desserts really sweet, pour a little clear honey on top of the dessert just before serving. The cream could be flavoured with a little brandy or blackcurrant liqueur if liked.

Orange Chiffon

Approximate preparation time: 15
minutes (plus standing time)
Serves 3

**3 large orange halves
150 ml/$\frac{1}{4}$ pint double cream
sherry to taste
mint or other edible leaves for
decoration**

Scoop out the orange flesh, being careful to leave the cases intact. Cut the edges of the orange into a series of points using a pair of small, very sharp scissors. Cut the bases of the orange cases level so that they will stand upright on the plate. Use the trimmings to make orange shreds for decoration.

Cut all the white pith off the orange flesh and reserve any juice that runs out. Discard the orange pips and pith.

Put the cream in a bowl; add most of the orange flesh, half the juice and the sherry. Whisk until thick and making soft peaks. Pile into the orange cases and chill for 4 hours. Decorate with orange slices, shredded rind and mint leaves.

Serve at once.

Sunset Sundae

Approximate preparation time: 10
minutes (plus standing time)
Cooking time: 7 minutes
Serves 4

**2 eggs
75 g/3 oz castor sugar
grated rind and juice of 1 medium
lemon
300 ml/$\frac{1}{2}$ pint single cream
300 ml/$\frac{1}{2}$ pint double cream
sliced Chinese gooseberries or
pears
sweet biscuits for serving**

Separate the eggs and beat the yolks with castor sugar until well mixed.

Very gradually add the lemon juice, half the rind and the single cream to the eggs. Put in the top of a double saucepan and stir until thick – be careful not to get it too hot or it may curdle.

Leave to cool. Whisk the egg whites until very stiff, then fold into the mixture. Spoon into four serving glasses and chill for 4 hours..

Whip the double cream, pile on top of the dessert, add the fruit and serve with the biscuits.

Variations

Instead of serving with biscuits, serve with tiny meringues dipped in chocolate. If you can get fresh figs they would be lovely in this cream and wine mixture – stir in lightly and top with whipped double cream.

Fruit with Iced Syllabub

Approximate preparation time: 10
minutes (plus standing time)
Serves 1

4 tablespoons single cream
4 tablespoons double cream
2 tablespoons sweet white wine
1 teaspoon sherry
1 teaspoon finely grated lemon rind
strawberries and slices of Chinese
gooseberry

Put the single and double creams in a bowl
with the wine, sherry and lemon rind. Whisk
slowly – don't use an electric mixer – until
the mixture starts to thicken. At this point
transfer the mixture to a serving glass with
the strawberries and slices of Chinese
gooseberry. Chill for 4 hours then serve.

Variations

If you can't get Chinese gooseberries – they
are usually available in this country from
July to February – substitute another unusual fruit such as passion fruit. These
should be available all the year. When you
cut open the fruit, take out the juicy pulp
and put in the bottom of the serving glass
before adding the syllabub mixture. You
could use the pulp of fresh figs in the same
way.

Pears in Snow

Approximate preparation time: 25
minutes
Cooking time: 50 minutes
Serves 5

5 medium pears (choose fairly ripe
ones)
juice of 1 small lemon
50 g/2 oz granulated sugar
150 ml/$\frac{1}{4}$ pint single cream
150 ml/$\frac{1}{4}$ pint double cream
2 tablespoons sweet white wine
plain chocolate, grated to decorate

Peel the pears using a stainless steel knife.
Remove the cores and stand in a shallow
ovenproof dish. Mix the lemon juice with
the sugar and 150 ml/$\frac{1}{4}$ pint water. Pour into
the dish with the pears. Cover the dish with
foil and cook in a moderate oven (180°C,
350°F, Gas Mark 4) for 50 minutes or until
tender. Leave to cool in the cooking liquid.

Whisk the single and double creams with
the wine. Turn into a serving dish and stand
the pears on top. Sprinkle with grated
chocolate.

Serve within 4 hours or the 'snow' will
start to collapse and the pears will discolour.

Variation

For an extra glossy finish, gently heat a little
apricot jam and then brush carefully over the
cooked pears as soon as they come out of
the oven. Leave to cool completely.

Coconut Sweet

Approximate preparation time: 20
minutes (plus standing time)
Cooking time: 45 minutes
Serves 3

3 large ripe bananas
juice of 1 small lemon
40 g/1$\frac{1}{2}$ oz butter
75 g/3 oz demerara or raw brown
sugar
75 g/3 oz coconut cream – or
desiccated coconut mixed with
double cream
1 large orange, sliced

Peel the bananas and arrange, whole in an
ovenproof dish. Sprinkle with the lemon
juice. Cut the butter in small pieces and
sprinkle over the bananas with the sugar.
Cook in a moderate oven (180°C, 350°F,
Gas Mark 4) for 45 minutes. Leave to cool.

Pipe or spoon the coconut cream over the
bananas. Chill then decorate with thin slices
of orange.

Variations
Replace the lemon juice with canned
orange juice and add a few sultanas. If you
don't want to use the oven, you can fry the
bananas. If they are very thick, cut them in
half lengthways and fry in a mixture of
butter and lemon juice. If you like a really
rich flavour, add some brandy and brown
sugar towards the end of frying. Chill them
thoroughly before serving. Serve within 4
hours of cooking.

Strawberry Cloud

Approximate preparation time: 20
minutes
Cooking time: 15 minutes
Serves 2

350 g/12 oz strawberries
1 large egg white
50 g/2 oz castor sugar

Halve the strawberries, reserving the best
ones for decoration. Arrange the rest in the
base of an ovenproof dish.

Whisk the egg white until stiff and standing in peaks. Add the sugar, whisking in 1
teaspoon at a time until the mixture is stiff
and shiny.

Pile the meringue over the strawberries
and cook in a moderately hot oven (200°C,
400°F, Gas Mark 6) for 15 minutes or until
pale golden. Cool, then arrange the remaining strawberries on top.

Serve within 3 hours.

Variations
If liked, use raspberries in place of the
strawberries. For a special occasion, flavour
some double cream with brandy or a fruit
liqueur to serve with the dessert.

You could use canned fruit, but be sure to
drain off the juice first. The slightly sharp
taste of pineapple goes well with the sweet
meringue or try well-drained canned
rhubarb or gooseberries. This is extra good
served with cream.

Sherry Fruit Salad

Approximate preparation time: 20
minutes
Cooking time: 5 minutes
Serves 4

1 very large orange
225 g/8 oz ripe red plums
100 g/4 oz sweet green grapes
100 g/4 oz black grapes
1 large banana
1 large red apple or a sweet green
apple
1 (227-g/8-oz) can pineapple cubes
or fresh pineapple
4 tablespoons sweet sherry
25 g/1 oz castor sugar
2 tablespoons lemon juice

Cut off the peel and the white pith, then slice the orange into thick rounds. Halve the plums and take out the stones. Peel the grapes. Peel and slice the banana. Don't peel the apple, just remove the core and cut the apple into chunks. Drain the pineapple, reserving a little of the syrup. If you are using fresh pineapple, peel it and cut into chunks – do this on a plate so you don't lose any of the juice. Toss the apple and banana in a little pineapple syrup or juice to prevent discoloration.

Put 300 ml/$\frac{1}{2}$ pint cold water in a small pan with the sherry, sugar and lemon juice. Heat gently until the sugar has dissolved, then boil for 2 minutes. Leave to cool, then pour over the fruit. Mix well and put in a serving bowl.

This will keep for up to 1 day in the lower part of the refrigerator.

Serve with fresh cream or chilled custard.

Variations
If you are using fresh pineapple, cut in half lengthways then remove the flesh, leaving the shell of the pineapple intact. Serve the fruit salad piled into the pinapple shells – it looks terrific. Serve with a jug of thick cream with finely grated lemon rind mixed in.

French Strawberry Sweet

Approximate preparation time: 10
minutes
Serves 2

1 (425-g/15-oz) can creamed rice
pudding, chilled
4 tablespoons single cream
225 g/8 oz strawberries
2 tablespoons brandy or sweet
sherry

Put the rice pudding in a bowl and mix in the cream.

Cut the strawberries in half and sprinkle the brandy or sherry over. Very gently mix the strawberries with the rice and spoon into serving glasses.

This can be served right away, or kept in the refrigerator for a couple of hours.

Variations
You could transform this pudding into a layer sweet. Crush some digestive biscuits and divide between 2 serving glasses. Add a layer of rice pudding, a layer of strawberries, then more biscuits. Continue the layers until all the ingredients are used up. Top with a swirl of whipped cream and a walnut. Tiny meringues could be stirred into the rice pudding with the strawberries; they add a nice crunch.

If you have enough time, you could put a layer of jelly at the base of the dessert. Lime goes particularly well with the strawberries. Pour the jelly into the glass and give it time to set before adding the rice mixture.

Accompaniments
Small sweet biscuits can be served with this dessert. The tiny iced diamond biscuits are particularly good, or stick some brandy snaps into the dessert just before serving so they don't go soggy. Fill the brandy snaps with whipped cream.

Cherry Rice

Approximate preparation time: 15
minutes (plus standing time)
Serves 4

**1 (425-g/15-oz) can creamed rice
pudding
2 teaspoons port
450 g/1 lb cherries**

Mix the rice pudding with the port and put
in the refrigerator to chill for 2 hours.

Leave the stalks on a few of the cherries.
Take the stalks off the rest and remove the
stones. Mix these cherries with the rice and
spoon into a glass serving bowl. Put the
cherries with the stalks on top for
decoration.

Variations
Soak the cherries in a little cherry brandy or
Kirsch before mixing with the rice. When
cherries are not in season, try a mixture of
glacé fruit with the rice and mix in some
cream to make it even richer.

Serve a little clear honey as a sauce.

Tropical Sweet

Approximate preparation time: 15
minutes
Serves 2–3

**2 large oranges
$\frac{1}{2}$ (227-g/8-oz) box dessert dates (not
compressed)
shredded coconut
1 glacé or fresh cherry for
decoration**

Peel the oranges and remove all the white
pith. Divide the oranges into segments and
put on a platter with the dates. Decorate
with the coconut and cherry.

Variations
When fresh dates are in season, it's worth
using them. Fresh coconut is good too. The
oranges take on a special flavour if you soak

them in coffee. To do this, peel the oranges,
cut into neat slices and put in a heatproof
dish. Heat 300 ml/$\frac{1}{2}$ pint water in a small pan
with 1 slightly rounded teaspoon instant
coffee and 25 g/1 oz castor sugar. Boil for 2
minutes. Pour over the oranges and leave to
stand for 4 hours then strain well. Serve with
fancy biscuits and cream flavoured with
orange liqueur and sprinkled with very
finely grated orange or lemon rind.

Melon Bowl

Approximate preparation time: 25
minutes (plus standing time)
Serves 2–3

**1 large ripe melon
175 g/6 oz strawberries
1 large banana
juice of 1 small lemon
2 tablespoons sweet sherry
1 teaspoon castor sugar
1 (170-g/6-oz) can evaporated milk,
chilled
2 tablespoons brandy**

Cut the top of the melon. Scoop out and
discard the seeds. Use a melon baller or
spoon to scoop out the melon flesh, leaving
the melon case intact.

Cut the strawberries in half. Peel and slice
the banana. Put the strawberries, banana
and melon in a bowl. Pour over the lemon
juice and sherry. Stir in the sugar until
dissolved.

Whip the evaporated milk until very thick,
then stir in the brandy. Spoon this into the
empty melon case and put the fruit mixture
on top. Chill for 5 hours, then serve.

Variations
For an even more refreshing dessert, leave
out the evaporated milk and fill the base of
the melon with lime jelly.

Brandied Melon

Approximate preparation time: 20
minutes (plus standing time)
Serves 4

1 large ripe melon (not
watermelon)
3 tablespoons brandy
50 g/2 oz castor sugar
225 g/8 oz raspberries
150 ml/$\frac{1}{4}$ pint double cream or small
meringues to decorate

Cut the top off the melon and scoop out the seeds. Use a melon baller, if you have one, to scoop out the flesh in balls, or use a teaspoon.

Put the melon balls and the juice from the melon in a bowl. Keep the melon case. Sprinkle the brandy and half the sugar over the melon in the bowl and leave to stand for 4 hours. Then pile the melon back into its case and add the raspberries. Sprinkle the remaining sugar on top.

Whip the cream until thick and pipe on top, or use the meringues to decorate.

Variations

If you don't want to serve the dessert in the melon case, spoon the melon balls and raspberries into wine glasses and pour in some single cream. For a very refreshing dessert, instead of cream, serve with raspberry sorbet or some lemon water ice.

Gooseberry Fool

Approximate preparation time: 20
minutes (plus standing time)
Cooking time: 15 minutes
Serves 4

300 ml/$\frac{1}{2}$ pint thick, cold custard
675 g/1$\frac{1}{2}$ lb gooseberries
115 g/4$\frac{1}{2}$ oz castor sugar
50 g/2 oz walnuts
1 (170-g/6-oz) can cream

Chill the custard in the refrigerator. Top, tail and wash the gooseberries. Put them in a pan with the sugar and 5 tablespoons water. Cover and simmer for 15 minutes, or until tender.

Put half the gooseberries to one side for decorating. Sieve the rest with the cooking liquid. Leave to cool then mix with the chilled custard.

Chop up half the walnuts very finely and mix into the custard. Stir in the cream and turn into a glass dish. Decorate with the whole gooseberries and the walnuts.

Variations

Cooked blackcurrants or redcurrants can replace the gooseberries – you may find you need less sugar with the currants. If liked use very ripe raspberries and strawberries, mashed to a purée and mixed into the custard. Serve within 4 hours.

Loganberry Towers

Approximate preparation time: 25
minutes (plus standing time)
Serves 8

2 (35-g/1$\frac{1}{4}$-oz) sachets vanilla
blancmange powder
50 g/2 oz castor sugar
600 ml/1 pint milk
600 ml/1 pint single cream
150 ml/$\frac{1}{4}$ pint double cream
450 g/1 lb loganberries
1 (227-g/8-oz) can peach slices
1 tablespoon rum or a few drops
rum essence

Put the blancmange powder and sugar in a
bowl and mix to a smooth paste with a little
of the milk. Heat the milk and single cream
until almost boiling then pour on to the
blancmange powder. Mix well then pour
back into pan and simmer, stirring, until
thick. Pour into eight small damped moulds
and leave to set.

When the blancmange has set, dip the
moulds in hot water for 5 seconds then turn
out and decorate with whipped cream and
loganberries. Surround the base of the
towers with the rest of the loganberries and
peach slices. Mix the syrup from the can
with the rum and pour around the dessert.
Serve within 4 hours.

Variations
Try chocolate-flavoured blancmange and
instead of loganberries and peaches, use
raspberries and a can of mandarin oranges.
If you don't have any small moulds, set the
mixture in a 1-litre/2-pint ring mould then
fill the centre with fruit and cream. Serve
within 4 hours of filling.

Strawberry Cream

Approximate preparation time: 20
minutes (plus standing time)
Serves 10

3 (425-g/15-oz) cans strawberries
25 g/1 oz powdered gelatine
300 ml/$\frac{1}{2}$ pint double cream
300 ml/$\frac{1}{2}$ pint single cream
6 large egg whites
cream, strawberries and angelica
for decoration

Sieve the strawberries with their syrup or
mash with a fork until smooth.

Put the gelatine in a small bowl with 4
tablespoons cold water. Stand in a bowl of
very hot water and leave until the gelatine
has dissolved. Then whisk, in a steady
stream, into the strawberry purée.

Mix the double and single creams together
and stir into the strawberries.

Whisk the egg whites until very stiff and
fold into the strawberry mixture using a
metal spoon. Put in a glass serving dish and
leave to set.

Decorate with cream, strawberries and
angelica and serve at once, or keep in the
refrigerator for up to 4 hours.

Variations
Purée stewed blackcurrants or gooseberries
and use instead of strawberries.

Pineapple Dream

Approximate preparation time: 5 minutes
Serves 2

1 (227-g/8-oz) can pineapple cubes
or fresh pineapple
1 (170-g/6-oz) can evaporated milk,
chilled
25 g/1 oz angelica
strawberries to decorate

Drain the pineapple and put in a glass dish. Whisk the milk until it is thick enough to stand up in soft peaks. The milk will only whip if it has been thoroughly chilled.

Chop the angelica into tiny pieces and mix with the evaporated milk; put on top of the pineapple than decorate with halved strawberries. Serve at once.

Variations
This can be turned into a lovely trifle. Put some trifle sponges or slices of chocolate Swiss roll into the bottom of the dish before adding the fruit. Moisten with a little juice from the can of pineapple. For a real treat, replace the angelica with glacé pineapple. This transforms the dessert into something special enough for a dinner party.

Citrus Cream

Approximate preparation time: 25 minutes (plus standing time)
Serves 3–4

1 small lemon
1 small orange
4 lumps sugar
3 tablespoons sweet white wine
1 tablespoon sweet sherry
150 ml/$\frac{1}{4}$ pint single cream
300 ml/$\frac{1}{2}$ pint double cream
20 sponge finger biscuits

Wash and dry the lemon and the orange. Rub the sugar lumps over the rind to soak up the zest. Put in a bowl. Squeeze and strain the lemon and orange juice.

Cut off a few strips of lemon peel; remove any white pith and put the peel in the bowl with the sugar lumps. Stir in the wine, sherry, 1 tablespoon lemon juice and 1 tablespoon orange juice. Leave to stand for 3 hours, then strain.

Put the wine mixture in a fresh bowl with the single and double creams. Whisk slowly (don't use an electric mixer) until very thick and starting to stand up in peaks.

Put the mixture in a large glass bowl and chill for up to 4 hours before serving. Not more than 30 minutes before serving, arrange the biscuits around the edge of the dish.

Fresh Cream Velvet

Approximate preparation time: 20 minutes
Serves 3

1$\frac{1}{2}$ teaspoons grated lemon rind
450 ml/$\frac{3}{4}$ pint double cream
3 teaspoons sweet sherry
1 tablespoon ground almonds
cream and raspberries for
decoration

Put the lemon rind in a bowl with the cream, sherry and almonds. Whisk gently until thick (don't use an electric mixer). Put the mixture in a shallow glass dish.

Whisk the extra cream and pipe it in rosettes around the edge of the dish, then add the raspberries.

Variations
Instead of using the raspberries, toast some blanched chopped almonds until golden and sprinkle over the top of the mixture. For a richer flavour, omit the sherry and use brandy or a fruit-flavoured liqueur. You could pick out the almond flavour by serving the desserts with some almond-flavoured biscuits or by decorating the top of the cream with sugared almonds instead of the raspberries – alternate the colours for a really pretty effect.

Apple Juice Syllabub

Approximate preparation time: 15
minutes (plus standing time)
Serves 3–4

4 tablespoons unsweetened apple
juice
150 ml/$\frac{1}{4}$ pint single cream
300 ml/$\frac{1}{2}$ pint double cream
1 tablespoon clear honey
bunches of green grapes for
decoration

Put the apple juice in a mixing bowl with the
single and double creams and honey. Whisk
gently (don't use an electric mixer) until the
mixture is just beginning to thicken and
stand up in peaks. Pour into a glass bowl.
Chill well in the refrigerator. Decorate with
tiny bunches of green grapes.
  Serve within 5 hours.

Seasonal fruits
*Make the most of fresh fruits when
they are plentiful.*
Blackberries: *must be used as soon as
you buy them, should be available
from August to October.*
Cranberries: *an American fruit with a
sharp flavour, available in December
and January.*
Blackcurrants: *almost always need
cooking and sweetening, available in
July and August.*
Gooseberries: *vary in flavour from
sweet to very sour, available from May
to August.*
Loganberries: *a mellow flavour
available in July and August.*
Raspberries: *less juicy, but with a
subtle flavour, available from July to
September.*
Redcurrants: *when ripe, lovely to eat
raw – a superb colour. Available in
July and August.*
Strawberries: *available from June to
July.*

Coffee Cream

Approximate preparation time: 25
minutes
Serves 4

75 g/3 oz plain dessert chocolate
300 ml/$\frac{1}{2}$ pint single cream
300 ml/$\frac{1}{2}$ pint double cream
1 teaspoon instant coffee powder
icing sugar (optional)
extra double cream for decoration
roasted hazelnuts
canned, glacé or fresh cherries
sponge finger biscuits or cigarette
biscuits

Start by making the chocolate curls; break
the chocolate into squares and put in a bowl
over a pan of gently simmering water. When
the chocolate has melted, pour on to a
perfectly clean laminated worktop. When
the chocolate has hardened, draw a sharp
knife across it towards you, the blade held at
an angle to shave the chocolate into curls.
  Whisk the single and double creams together until just beginning to thicken (don't
use an electric mixer). Fold in the coffee
using a metal spoon. Taste and add sugar, if
you think it needs it, just a little at a time. Put
the mixture in a glass serving bowl.
  Whip the extra cream until thick and pipe
on top of the coffee mixture. Add the
cherries, hazelnuts and chocolate curls.
Surround the dish with the sponge finger
biscuits and cherries.
  Serve within 3 hours.

Variation
If you have any cherry brandy, sprinkle it
over fresh cherries. Leave for 2 hours to
absorb the flavour and serve as a topping for
the cream (add just before serving).

Coffee Whip

Approximate preparation time: 15
minutes
Serves 3

150 ml/$\frac{1}{4}$ pint single cream
150 ml/$\frac{1}{4}$ pint double cream
1 tablespoon castor sugar
2 teaspoons very finely ground
coffee or instant coffee powder
1 teaspoon brandy
extra double cream and coffee
beans for decoration

Put the single and double creams in a large
mixing bowl with the sugar and coffee.
Whisk slowly and carefully, using a balloon
or rotary whisk (don't use an electric mixer).
Stir in the brandy. When the mixture is thick,
spoon into three wine glasses or glass
dishes. Decorate with the extra cream and
coffee beans.

Serve at once, or keep in the lower part of
refrigerator for up to 4 hours.

Variations
Try adding a little rum instead of brandy to
the coffee mixture; add it drop by drop to the
whisked mixture, stirring it in with a spoon.
Sprinkle plain grated chocolate on top,
instead of coffee beans. You could serve the
coffee whip with a milk chocolate flake bar,
stuck in the glass just before serving, or
serve with cigarette biscuits or brandy
snaps.

German Cream Cheese Sweet

Approximate preparation time: 15
minutes (plus standing time)
Serves 2

225 g/8 oz cream cheese
2$\frac{1}{2}$ tablespoons single cream
40 g/1$\frac{1}{2}$ oz castor sugar
1 egg yolk
few drops vanilla essence
black cherry jam for topping

Put the cream cheese in a mixing bowl with
the cream, sugar, egg yolk and vanilla essence. Beat until well mixed but don't over-
beat. Chill well then spoon or pipe into two
serving glasses.

Pile the jam on top and serve at once.

Cream cheese notes
*As its name suggests, it is made from
the cream of the milk and has a high fat
content. Double cream cheese has a
fat content of 45 to 50 per cent and
needs no rennet to help it set. Single
cream cheese is 25 to 30 per cent fat
and is made with rennet.*

*Like cream, this cheese should only
be kept for 2 days and must be stored
in the refrigerator. You can buy it loose
from delicatessens, or you can buy the
brand-name wrapped cheeses.*

*Don't try to substitute cottage or
curd cheese for cream cheese; these
are both unsuitable for the cream
cheese recipe on this page although
they are sometimes used in cheese-
cakes.*

Rum Cups

Approximate preparation time: 15 minutes (plus standing time)
Cooking time: 5 minutes
Serves 2

$\frac{1}{2}$ (35-g/1$\frac{1}{4}$-oz) sachet chocolate
blancmange powder
15 g/$\frac{1}{2}$ oz castor sugar
1$\frac{1}{2}$ teaspoons cocoa powder
150 ml/$\frac{1}{4}$ pint milk
150 ml/$\frac{1}{4}$ pint evaporated milk
few drops rum essence
2 canned pear halves
150 ml/$\frac{1}{4}$ pint double cream
walnut halves for decoration

Mix the blancmange powder with the sugar and cocoa, then follow instructions on the packet, using the fresh and evaporated milk to make up the 300 ml/$\frac{1}{2}$ pint liquid. Flavour with a few drops of rum essence being careful not to add too much.

When the blancmange is warm, but not setting, pour into two large wine glasses or glass dishes. Cover with cling film to prevent a skin forming, and leave to set in cool place or in the refrigerator.

Add the pear halves, whipped cream and walnut halves.

Serve immediately or keep in the refrigerator for 3 hours.

Variations
Experiment with different fruits. Ones that are particularly good with the chocolate blancmange are fresh apricots, peaches and raspberries. Instead of using whipped cream, decorate the top of the blancmange with tiny meringues – these keep very well if stored in an airtight tin.

Apricot Mould

Approximate preparation time: 10 minutes (plus standing time)
Cooking time: 5 minutes
Serves 4

1 (35-g/1$\frac{1}{4}$-oz) sachet vanilla
blancmange powder
50 g/2 oz castor sugar
600 ml/1 pint milk
1 small egg yolk
1 (425-g/15-oz) can apricot halves

Mix the blancmange powder and the sugar with a little of the milk. Bring the rest of milk to the boil then pour on to the blancmange. Mix well, return to the pan and simmer, stirring all the time for 2 minutes or until thick – be careful not to overcook it.

Take the pan off the heat and beat in the egg yolk. Chop up three apricot halves fairly finely and stir into the mixture. Wet a mould. Pour in the mixture and leave to set in the refrigerator.

When set, dip the mould in hot water for 5 seconds, then turn out on to a serving plate. Surround with the remaining apricots.

Variations
Other canned fruit can be used in place of the apricots; choose firm ones, so you get a speckled effect. If liked pour single cream over the mould just before serving.

Italian Mould

Approximate preparation time: 30
minutes (plus standing time)
Cooking time: 2 minutes
Serves 8

2 (600-ml/1-pint) packets orange
jelly
15 g/$\frac{1}{2}$ oz powdered gelatine
600 ml/1 pint very fresh milk
150 ml/$\frac{1}{4}$ pint single cream
1 small orange
orange, raspberry or strawberry
leaves for decoration
150 ml/$\frac{1}{4}$ pint double cream for
decoration

Break the jelly into cubes and put in a
saucepan with 1.15 litres/2 pints water.
Sprinkle gelatine over the top and stir over a
low heat until dissolved.

When the jelly mixture is cool, but not
setting, mix in milk and single cream.

Wet a 1.75-litre/3-pint fancy jelly mould.
Pour in the jelly and leave to set in a cool
place.

When the jelly has set, dip the mould in
hot water for 5 seconds then turn out on to a
serving plate.

Cut the orange in segments and use to
decorate the mould. Add the edible leaves
(do make very sure they are edible). Whip
the double cream until thick and pipe
around the base of the mould.

Serve the same day.

Variations
Experiment with different flavours of jelly –
but always match the fruit garnish with the
flavour of the jelly. You can set the jellies in
individual dishes, then top each one with a
swirl of cream and a small piece of fruit or
serve with vanilla ice cream.

Maraschino Mould

Approximate preparation time: 20
minutes (plus standing time)
Cooking time: 2 minutes
Serves 4

20 g/$\frac{3}{4}$ oz powdered gelatine
600 ml/1 pint creamy milk
25 g/1 oz castor sugar
2 large eggs
1 (113-g/4-oz) jar red maraschino
cherries

Put the gelatine in a small bowl with 4
tablespoons cold water. Stand the bowl in a
pan of very hot water until the gelatine has
dissolved completely.

Heat the milk with the sugar until almost
boiling. Take off the heat. Separate the eggs
and beat the yolks into the hot milk. Mix in
the dissolved gelatine. Leave until just beginning to set.

Whisk the egg whites until stiff, then fold
into the mixture using a metal spoon. Rinse a
1-litre/1$\frac{1}{2}$ pint jelly mould with cold water.
Pour in the milk mixture and leave to set.
When set, dip the mould in hot water for 5
seconds, and turn out on to a serving plate.
Decorate with the cherries and their juice.

Serve the same day.

Variations
Small strawberries tossed in sugar can replace the cherries. To delight the younger
members of the family, set the mixture in
individual moulds – or use a large 'rabbit'
shaped mould and decorate with chocolate
buttons.

Rice Cake

Approximate preparation time: 25
minutes (plus standing time)
Serves 4

1 (425-g/15-oz) can creamed rice
pudding
150 ml/$\frac{1}{4}$ pint single cream
brandy to taste
15 g/$\frac{1}{2}$ oz powdered gelatine
25 g/1 oz icing sugar
mixed chopped glacé fruits and
angelica for decoration

Mix the rice pudding with the cream and
add brandy to taste.

Put the gelatine in a small bowl with 2
tablespoons cold water. Stand the bowl in a
pan of very hot water until the gelatine has
dissolved completely. Cool then stir into the
rice.

Wet a deep 13-cm/5-inch cake tin. Pour
in the rice mixture and leave to set. Losen the
edges with fingers. Dip the tin in hot water
for 5 seconds and turn out on to a serving
dish.

Sift the icing sugar and mix with just
enough water to make a thin coating of
icing. Quickly pour over the rice cake and
leave to set in a cool place.

Decorate the cake with glacé fruits and
angelica.

Eat the same day.

Variation
Replace the icing with whipped cream.

Raspberry Ring

Approximate preparation time: 20
minutes (plus standing time)
Cooking time: 2 minutes
Serves 4–5

20 g/$\frac{3}{4}$ oz powdered gelatine
2 medium oranges
450 ml/$\frac{3}{4}$ pint milk
3 eggs
100 g/4 oz castor sugar
1 teaspoon cornflour
$\frac{1}{2}$ (170-g/6-oz) can evaporated milk
225 g/8 oz raspberries
300 ml/$\frac{1}{2}$ pint double cream

Put the gelatine in a small bowl with 2
tablespoons cold water. Stand the bowl in a
pan of very hot water and leave until the
gelatine has dissolved.

Finely grate the rind from 1 orange and
put in a saucepan with the fresh milk.

Halve the ungrated orange and use half
for decoration. Squeeze and strain the juice
from other half, and from the grated orange.
Mix the orange juice with the gelatine.
Whisk the eggs with the sugar and cornflour
until creamy.

Heat the fresh milk until almost boiling
and stir into the egg mixture. Mix in the
orange juice and gelatine, and leave to cool.
When it starts to set, stir in the evaporated
milk. Wet an 18-cm/7-inch ring mould. Pour
the mixture into the ring and leave to set.
Dip the mould in hot water for 5 seconds
then turn out. Fill the centre with raspberries. Whip the cream and use with the
orange to decorate the mould.

Serve within 3 hours.

White Wine Jelly

Approximate preparation time: 20
minutes (plus standing time)
Cooking time: 2 minutes
Serves 6

**1 bottle Moselle wine
1 (5-cm/2-inch) stick cinnamon
75 g/3 oz castor sugar
20 g/$\frac{3}{4}$ oz powdered gelatine
225 g/8 oz sweet green grapes
1 small egg white
castor sugar
whipped cream for decoration**

Pour the wine into a saucepan; add the cinnamon and two-thirds of the sugar. Heat gently without boiling. Strain the hot wine into a heatproof jug.

Put the gelatine in a small bowl with 4 tablespoons cold water. Stand the bowl in a pan of very hot water and leave until the gelatine has dissolved. Stir into the wine.

Put two-thirds of the grapes in hot water for a minute – this will make them easy to peel. Peel the grapes; cut in half and remove the pips.

Wet a 20-cm/8-inch ring mould. Pour a little of the wine mixture into the base and leave to set. Add a layer of grapes, then a little more jelly and leave to set. Repeat until the ingredients are all used up. When completely set, turn out and decorate with whole grapes tossed in egg white and sugar. Pipe stars of whipped cream around the base.

Serve within 3 hours.

Old-fashioned Milk Mould

Approximate preparation time: 20 minutes (plus standing time)
Cooking time: 5 minutes
Serves 5

40 g/1½ oz cornflour
600 ml/1 pint creamy milk
few drops almond essence
few drops edible pink food colouring
25 g/1 oz butter
whipped cream and angelica for decoration

Wet a 1-litre/1½-pint jelly mould.

Put the cornflour in a bowl with 5 tablespoons of the milk and mix to a smooth paste. Flavour the rest of the milk with almond essence and add a little pink colouring. Bring to the boil and pour on to the cornflour mixture. Mix well, then pour back into the pan. Simmer gently, stirring all the time, for about 2 minutes or until thick.

Remove from the heat and beat in the butter – this will give it a nice shine. Pour into the jelly mould and leave to set. When set, dip the mould in hot water for 5 seconds, then turn out on to a pretty serving plate. Decorate with cream and angelica.

Variations
Instead of using a jelly mould, set the mixture in a ring mould, then fill the centre with a mixture of colourful fresh fruit.

Summer Snow Mould

Approximate preparation time: 15
minutes (plus standing time)
Cooking time: 2 minutes
Serves 3–4

50 g/2 oz castor sugar
2 thin strips lemon rind
450 ml /$\frac{3}{4}$ pint milk
15 g/$\frac{1}{2}$ oz gelatine
300 ml/$\frac{1}{2}$ pint single cream

Put the sugar in a small saucepan with the lemon rind and milk. Heat gently until the sugar dissolves, then leave to stand for 10 minutes. Strain and leave to cool.

Put the gelatine in a small bowl with 4 tablespoons cold water. Stand the bowl in a pan of very hot water until the gelatine has dissolved completely. Mix with the milk and half the cream.

Wet a 600-ml/1-pint jelly mould. Pour in the milk mixture and leave to set. When it has set, dip the mould in very hot water for 5 seconds and turn out. Pour the remaining cream over the top.

Eat the same day.

Accompaniments
Serve the mould with fruit. Stewed blackcurrants, thoroughly chilled, or a purée of cooked and chilled gooseberries served as a sauce are both very good with the mould.

Almond Ring

Approximate preparation time: 20
minutes (plus standing time)
Serves 6

35 g/1$\frac{1}{4}$ oz powdered gelatine
600 ml/1 pint milk
600 ml/1 pint single cream
few drops almond essence
few drops yellow food colouring
1 (425-g/15-oz) can peach slices

Put the gelatine in a small bowl with 5 tablespoons cold water. Stand the bowl in a pan of very hot water until the gelatine has dissolved. Cool a little then mix with the milk and cream. Flavour with almond essence and add a little colouring.

Wet a 1.25-litre/2-pint ring mould. Pour in the milk mixture and leave to set.

When set, dip the mould in hot water for 5 seconds then turn out on to a serving plate. Arrange the peach slices round base.

Variations
Fill the centre of the ring with whipped cream and sprinkle with some lightly toasted, chopped almonds. Use slices of red-skinned apple in place of the canned fruit and pipe cream between the apple slices all round the base of the ring:

Serve within 4 hours of adding the cream.

Dairy Jelly

Approximate preparation time: 20
minutes (plus standing time)
Serves 4

15 g/$\frac{1}{2}$ oz powdered gelatine
450 ml/$\frac{3}{4}$ pint creamy milk
150 ml/$\frac{1}{4}$ pint single cream
few drops lemon essence
icing sugar to taste
150 ml/$\frac{1}{4}$ pint double cream
1 small banana
25 g/1 oz blanched almonds
1 slice of lemon

Put the gelatine in a small bowl with 4
tablespoons cold water. Stand the bowl in a
pan of very hot water until the gelatine has
dissolved completely.

Mix the milk with the single cream and stir
in the dissolved gelatine; add lemon essence and sugar to taste.

Wet a 600-ml/1-pint jelly mould. Pour the
milk mixture into the mould and leave to set.
When set, dip the mould in hot water for 5
seconds, then turn out on to a serving plate.

Whisk the double cream until thick. Pipe
rosettes of cream round the jelly and place
slices of banana between them.

Chop the almonds and toast lightly under
the grill – watch them all the time as they
burn quite quickly. Use to decorate the jelly
with the slice of lemon.

Variation
For a more elaborate dessert, surround the
jelly with ripe redcurrants.

Two-flavour Jelly

Approximate preparation time: 20
minutes (plus standing time)
Cooking time: 2 minutes
Serves 6–8

35 g/1$\frac{1}{4}$ oz powdered gelatine
1.15 litres/2 pints creamy milk
3 teaspoons instant coffee powder
50 g/2 oz castor sugar
orange segments for decoration

Put half the gelatine in one small bowl and
the other half in another. Put 4 tablespoons
water in each bowl. Stand the bowls in a
pan of very hot water until the gelatine has
dissolved completely.

Heat half the milk with the coffee and half
the sugar until dissolved. Heat the remaining milk and sugar. Leave both to cool.

Add one lot of gelatine to the coffee milk
and one lot to the plain milk. Strain into
separate basins.

Wet a 1.25-litre/2-pint jelly mould. Pour
half the milk jelly into the mould. Let it set,
then pour in half the coffee jelly. Add
another layer of each in the same way. Heat
the mixtures if necessary.

Leave to set, then dip the mould in hot
water for 5 seconds and turn out. Decorate
with segments of fresh orange.

Serve the same day, keeping it cool.

Fluffy Lemon Soufflé

Approximate preparation time:
20 minutes (plus standing time)
Serves 5

15 g/$\frac{1}{2}$ oz powdered gelatine
grated rind of 1 and juice of 2
lemons
100 g/4 oz castor sugar
150 ml/$\frac{1}{4}$ pint double cream
4 tablespoons single cream
4 large eggs, separated
2 tablespoons top of the milk
whipped cream and chocolate
vermicelli to decorate

Tie a band of greaseproof paper around the outside of a 14-cm/5-inch soufflé dish, making a 10-cm/4-inch collar above the top of the dish. Brush the inside of the paper with corn oil.

Dissolve the gelatine in 4 tablespoons cold water in a small bowl in a pan of hot water.

Whisk the egg yolks with the sugar until thick and the mixture will hold the impression of the whisk for 5 seconds. Whisk the double cream with the single cream and whip the egg whites until stiff.

Fold the lemon juice, rind and top of the milk into the whisked yolks and stir in the gelatine, adding it in a thin stream and stirring all the time. Fold in the cream and egg whites using a metal spoon. Turn the mixture into the soufflé dish and smooth the top with a palette knife.

When set, remove the paper carefully and decorate the top with the whipped cream and chocolate vermicelli.

Keep in a cool place and eat the same day.

Blackberry Soufflé

Approximate preparation time:
20 minutes (plus standing time)

15 g/$\frac{1}{2}$ oz powdered gelatine
175 g/6 oz blackberries, cooked and
sweetened
4 large eggs, separated
100 g/4 oz castor sugar
150 ml/$\frac{1}{4}$ pint double cream
4 tablespoons single cream
2 tablespoons top of the milk
whipped cream and a few whole
blackberries to decorate

Tie a band of greaseproof paper around the outside of a 14-cm/5$\frac{1}{2}$-inch soufflé dish, making a 10-cm/4-inch collar above the top of the dish. Brush the inside of the paper with corn oil.

Dissolve the gelatine in 4 tablespoons water in a small bowl in a pan of hot water. Drain all the juice from the cooked blackberries.

Whisk the egg yolks with the sugar until the mixture holds the impression of the whisk for 5 seconds.

Whisk the egg whites and lightly whip the double cream with the single cream and milk. Add the dissolved gelatine to the egg yolk mixture in a thin stream, stirring all the time. Fold in the blackberries, cream mixture and the egg whites using a metal spoon.

Turn the mixture into the soufflé dish and leave to set.

Carefully remove the paper and decorate the soufflé with the cream and reserved blackberries.

Keep in a cool place and eat the same day.

Blackberry Soufflé

Mocha Soufflé

Approximate preparation time: 20
minutes (plus standing time)
Serves 3–4

15 g/$\frac{1}{2}$ oz powdered gelatine
4 tablespoons strong, cold black
coffee
4 large eggs
100 g/4 oz castor sugar
150 ml/$\frac{1}{4}$ pint double cream
4 tablespoons single cream
2 tablespoons creamy milk
chocolate vermicelli for decoration

Tie a band of greaseproof paper round the
outside of a 15 cm/6-inch soufflé dish. It
should be deep enough to make a
10 cm/4 inch collar above the rim of the
dish. Lightly oil the inside of the collar,
using a tasteless oil such as corn oil.

Put the gelatine in a small bowl with 4
tablespoons coffee. Stand the bowl in a pan
of very hot water until the gelatine has
dissolved completely.

Separate the eggs and whisk the yolks
with the sugar until the mixture is thick
enough to hold the impression of the whisk
for 5 seconds.

Lightly whisk the double and single
creams together with the creamy milk.
Whisk the egg whites until very stiff.

Pour the gelatine into the egg yolk mix-
ture in a steady stream, stirring all the time.
Fold in the whipped cream and egg whites.
Turn into the soufflé dish; leave to set.

Decorate the side of soufflé with chocolate vermicelli.

Eat the same day.

Hazelnut Soufflé

Approximate preparation time: 25
minutes (plus standing time)
Serves 3–4

15 g/$\frac{1}{2}$ oz powdered gelatine
4 large eggs
100 g/4 oz castor sugar
150 ml/$\frac{1}{4}$ pint double cream
4 tablespoons single cream
2 tablespoons creamy milk
75 g/3 oz hazelnuts, roasted and
finely chopped
whipped cream and whole
hazelnuts for decoration

Tie a band of greaseproof paper round the
outside of a 15-cm/6-inch soufflé dish. The
greaseproof should be deep enough to
make a 10-cm/4-inch collar above the rim of
the dish. Lightly oil the inside of the collar
with tasteless corn oil.

Put the gelatine in a small bowl with 4
tablespoons cold water. Stand the bowl in a
pan of very hot water until the gelatine has
dissolved completely.

Separate the eggs and whisk the yolks
with the sugar until thick enough to hold the
impression of the whisk for 5 seconds.

Whip the double cream with the single
cream and milk. Whisk the egg whites until
very stiff.

Add the gelatine to the egg yolk mixture
in a steady stream, stirring all the time. Fold
in 25 g/1 oz of the chopped hazelnuts, the
cream mixture and egg whites. Pour into the
soufflé dish and leave to set.

When set, carefully remove the paper and
press the remaining chopped nuts on the
side of the soufflé. Decorate with cream and
whole nuts.

Eat the same day.

Cherry Shortbread

Approximate preparation time: 20 minutes (plus standing time)
Serves 4–6

1 (600-ml/1-pint) packet strawberry jelly
300 ml/$\frac{1}{2}$ pint boiling water
scant 300 ml/$\frac{1}{2}$ pint milk
6 triangles shortbread
150 ml/$\frac{1}{4}$ pint double cream
1 (227-g/8-oz) can red cherries or glacé cherries

Dissolve the jelly in 300 ml/$\frac{1}{2}$ pint boiling water. When cool, but not set stir in enough of the milk to make up to 1 pint.

Rinse a 20-cm/8-inch flan dish, pour in the milk jelly and leave to set. When set, dip the dish in hot water for 5 seconds, then turn out on to a plate.

Top with the shortbread, whipped cream and cherries. Put the extra cherries round the base of the jelly.

Variations

When fresh strawberries are cheap and plentiful, put some in the jelly before it sets, then decorate the top with firm, whole strawberries. If there isn't time to make jelly, a thick fruity yogurt could go under the shortbread, with a fruit decoration to match the flavour that you choose. Serve straight away or the shortbread may become soggy.

Charlotte Russe

Approximate preparation time: 30 minutes (plus standing time)
Serves 4–6

$\frac{1}{2}$ jam sponge cake
2 tablespoons sweet sherry
50 g/2 oz icing sugar
20 sponge finger biscuits
2 large bananas
juice of 1 small lemon
1 (227-g/8-oz) can pineapple cubes
$\frac{1}{2}$ (600-ml/1-pint) packet lemon jelly
3 glacé cherries
angelica
extra jelly for decoration

This is a simple way to make a Charlotte Russe and one that does not need the special tin. Put the single layer of cake on a serving plate and sprinkle the sherry on the top. Mix the icing sugar with a little water to make a stiff icing.

Trim the biscuits and use the icing to stick them all round the cake – like a circular fence. Leave to set.

Peel and slice the bananas; toss them in lemon juice and put on the cake with the drained pineapple. Make up the jelly, following the directions on the packet. Keep back a little. When the jelly starts to set, not before, pour most of it over the fruit. Leave to set.

When the jelly has set, arrange the cherries and angelica on top. Gently heat the remaining jelly, just to melt it, and pour over the cherries and angelica to make a glaze. Leave to set.

Chop the extra jelly and arrange around the Charlotte Russe.

Traditionally, a gold ribbon is tied round the Charlotte Russe.

Serve within 4 hours.

Grapefruit Meringue

Approximate preparation time: 15
minutes
Cooking time: 20 minutes
Serves 4

1 large grapefruit
½ chocolate Swiss roll
2 tablespoons grapefruit or ginger
marmalade
2 large egg whites
100 g/4 oz castor sugar
angelica for decoration

Cut the grapefruit in half and very carefully remove the segments, keeping them intact. Shred a little rind for decoration.

Cut the Swiss roll into thick slices and put them in the centre of an ovenproof plate. Spread the marmalade over the slices of Swiss roll to cover.

Put the egg whites in a clean, dry bowl and whisk until very stiff. Whisk in half the sugar, adding it a teaspoon at a time. Keep on whisking until very stiff and standing in peaks. Fold in the remaining sugar and pipe or spoon over the Swiss roll slices, making sure they are completely covered.

Cook in a moderate oven (180°C, 350°F, Gas Mark 4) for 20 minutes, or until pale golden. Leave to cool. Decorate with the grapefruit segments, rind and angelica.

Serve within 4 hours or the meringue may collapse.

Peanut Trifle

Approximate preparation time: 15
minutes
Cooking time: 5 minutes
Serves 4

1 (425-g/15-oz) can mandarin
oranges
$\frac{1}{2}$ cup sweetened orange juice
2 teaspoons cornflour
1 (142-ml/5-fl oz) carton
strawberry-flavoured yogurt
4 tablespoons double cream
50 g/2 oz peanut brittle

Reserve about 16 orange segments to decorate the trifle. Sieve or liquidise the rest
and mix with the orange juice. Mix the
cornflour with a little orange juice and bring
the rest to the boil. Add to the cornflour,
return to the pan and cook, stirring, until
thick. Cool.

Pour into a glass serving dish. Mix the
yogurt with the cream and put on top of the
orange mixture.

Chop the peanut brittle and use to decorate the trifle, then add the orange.

Variations
You can experiment with other canned
fruits and yogurts, for example, apricots
with orange-flavoured yogurt or pears with
chocolate-flavoured yogurt – and use the
syrup from the canned fruit instead of
orange juice. For a more substantial trifle
add a layer of sponge cake at the bottom of
the dish and spread with strawberry jam.

Blackcurrant Trifle

Approximate preparation time: 20 minutes
Cooking time: 20 minutes
Serves 4–5

675 g/1½ lb blackcurrants
75 g/3 oz castor sugar
1 teaspoon arrowroot
3 trifle sponges
4 tablespoons blackcurrant jam
3 tablespoons whisky or rum
300 ml/½ pint double cream
4 tablespoons single cream

Prepare and wash the blackcurrants. Put them in a pan with the sugar and 5 table-spoons cold water. Cover and simmer gently for 15 minutes, or until tender. Drain off the juice. Stir the arrowroot with a little water, stir in the hot juice and pour into a saucepan. Cook, stirring, until thick. Put the fruit back in the thickened juice and leave to cool completely.

Cut the sponges in half and spread with the jam. Sprinkle the whisky or rum on top. Put the sponges in the base of a glass dish and put half the blackcurrants on top, to cover them completely.

Whisk the double and single creams together. Save a little for piping and put the rest on top of the blackcurrants in the dish. Smooth the top with a palette knife.

Decorate the edge of trifle with piped cream and put the remaining blackcurrants in the centre.

Variations
Fresh gooseberries or raspberries can be used instead of blackcurrants.

Grape Trifle

Approximate preparation time: 25 minutes
Cooking time: 5 minutes
Serves 4

1 (35-g/1¼-oz) sachet custard powder
600 ml/1 pint milk
40 g/1½ oz castor sugar
1 (425-g/15-oz) can pear halves
2 tablespoons brandy
100 g/4 oz green grapes
175 g/6 oz black grapes
3 tablespoons sweetened orange juice

Mix the custard powder with a little of the milk. Bring the remaining milk to the boil and pour into the custard powder. Stir well, return to the pan and cook, stirring until thick. Beat in the sugar.

Drain the pears, chop and mix with the brandy. Place in a glass serving dish. Put the green grapes on top of the pears. Divide the black grapes into small bunches. Keep most of them for the top of the trifle and put the remainder in the dish.

Pour the orange juice into the dish and top with the custard. Cover with cling film and leave to cool. Decorate with the black grapes.

Ginger Cake Trifle

Approximate preparation time: 20
minutes
Serves 4

1 small oblong ginger cake
3 tablespoons ginger marmalade
450 ml/$\frac{3}{4}$ pint cold, thick custard
1 (312-g/11-oz) can mandarin
oranges
150 ml/$\frac{1}{4}$ pint double cream
150 ml/$\frac{1}{4}$ pint single cream

Slice the cake and sandwich the pieces together with the marmalade. Place in a glass serving dish. Spoon the cold custard on top and smooth with a palette knife.

Drain the syrup from the oranges, this will not be needed. Put the fruit on top of the custard. Whisk the double and single creams together until slightly thickened, then pour into the dish.

Serve the same day.

Variations
If your family are not keen on the flavour of ginger, use Madeira cake and orange marmalade. Using the basic method in this recipe, you can experiment with different canned fruits and any of the following toppings:

Topping One: peak up the cream with the blade of a knife and sprinkle hundreds and thousands over the top.

Topping Two: alternate slices of crystallised orange and lemon all round the edge of the dish, after adding the cream.

Topping Three: make swirls over the top of the cream with chocolate dessert sauce straight from the tube.

Topping Four: use bought hard butterscotch toffee. Use a rolling pin to crush it fairly finely, then scatter over the top of the trifle.

Topping Five: buy some tiny jelly sweets and use them to make an attractive zig-zag pattern over the top of the cream.

Chocolate Rounds

Approximate preparation time: 10
minutes
Serves 5

300 ml/$\frac{1}{2}$ pint evaporated milk,
chilled
2 teaspoons lemon juice
5 thick slices chocolate Swiss roll
1 (425-g/15-oz) can apricot halves
2 tablespoons sherry or sweet
white wine

The milk must be thoroughly chilled or it will not thicken. Whisk the milk until it is thick but not too stiff. Mix in the lemon juice.

Divide the Swiss roll slices between two dishes, or use a small dish for each slice, Drain the juice from the apricots, pour most of it over the Swiss roll slices and let it soak in. Sprinkle the sherry or wine on top.

Spoon the thickened milk over the Swiss roll slices, then add the apricots.

Serve within 1 hour of assembling.

Variations
For a less rich flavour, instead of chocolate Swiss roll, use a plain jam-filled Swiss roll and omit the sherry. If you prefer to use fresh fruit, a mixture of banana slices and grapes would be good, or sweet mandarin oranges with thin slices of green dessert apples.

Summer Pudding

Approximate preparation time:
15 minutes
Cooking time: 5 minutes
Serves 4–6

15 g/$\frac{1}{2}$ oz butter
8–10 slices white bread
675 g/1$\frac{1}{2}$ lb mixed summer fruit
(raspberries, redcurrants,
strawberries, cherries,
blackcurrants)
4 tablespoons clear honey
150 ml/$\frac{1}{4}$ pint double cream

Use the butter to grease a 1.25-litre/2-pint pudding basin. Cut the crusts from the bread and use the slices to line the basin, covering the sides and the bottom.

Prepare the fruit according to its type and place in a saucepan with the honey. Simmer gently until the juices flow. Strain off some of the juice and pour over the bread lining.

Pour half the fruit into the basin then add a layer of bread. Add the rest of the fruit and cover with a layer of bread. Place a small plate on top of the pudding, making sure it is resting on the pudding, not the sides of the basin. Put a weight on the plate and leave in the refrigerator overnight.

Turn the pudding out on to a serving dish and whip the cream. Use the cream to decorate the pudding.

Variations
On very hot days, replace the cream with home-made ice cream or try a different flavour such as coffee or fruit.

Peach Pavlova

Approximate preparation time: 30 minutes
Cooking time: 1 hour
Serves 3

1 teaspoon cornfour
1 teaspoon vanilla essence
1 teaspoon distilled malt vinegar
3 egg whites
200 g/7 oz castor sugar
150 ml/$\frac{1}{4}$ pint double cream
1 (425-g/15-oz) can peach halves

Line a baking tray with parchment paper or foil.

Mix the cornflour with the vanilla essence and vinegar. In another bowl, whisk the egg whites until very stiff. Whisk in the sugar, a teaspoon at a time, adding the cornflour mixture as you go. The mixture must be very stiff.

Pipe or spoon the meringue on to the prepared baking sheet or make a nest shape.

Put the meringue in a cool oven (140°C, 275°F, Gas Mark 1) and immediately turn down to very cool (120°C, 250°F, Gas Mark $\frac{1}{2}$) for 1 hour then turn the oven off and leave the meringue in until cool.

Put the cold meringue on a serving plate. Whip the cream and use to fill the centre with the drained peaches.

Variation
Flavour the whipped cream with peach brandy or a fruit liqueur.

Summer Pudding

Pasta Banana Cake

Approximate preparation time: 10
minutes (plus chilling time)
Cooking time: 35–40 minutes
Serves 6

150 g/5 oz short-cut pasta
5 eggs
75 g/3 oz castor sugar
300 ml/$\frac{1}{2}$ pint milk
300 ml/$\frac{1}{2}$ pint double cream
3 large bananas
demerara sugar to sprinkle

Cook the pasta in boiling water for 10
minutes or until just tender. Drain
thoroughly.

Whisk the eggs and sugar together over a
pan of hot, but not boiling, water until thick,
light and creamy. Gently heat the milk with
the cream and whisk into the egg yolks and
sugar. Put the custard mixture in the top of a
double saucepan and stir over a moderate
heat for 20–25 minutes or until the custard is
thick enough to coat the back of a wooden
spoon.

Remove from the heat and stir in the
cooked pasta. Pour into a shallow ovenproof dish and leave to cool. Slice the
bananas and arrange over the pasta with a
generous layer of demerara sugar. Put under
a hot grill until the sugar caramelises. Cool,
then chill for about 4 hours before serving.

Variations
Thin slices of orange can replace the bananas. Make sure you get rid of all the white
pith when you peel the oranges. Some
chocolate curls or finely grated chocolate
can be sprinkled on top of the pudding after
it has been chilled or, if liked, cover the dish
with thick cream.

Scandinavian Apple Cake

Approximate preparation time: 20
minutes
Cooking time: 13 minutes
Serves 4

675 g/1$\frac{1}{2}$ lb cooking apples
1 large orange
75 g/3 oz soft brown sugar
300 ml/$\frac{1}{2}$ pint double cream
40 g/1$\frac{1}{2}$ oz butter
1 tablespoon corn oil
2 cups fresh white breadcrumbs

Peel and core the apples, cut into chunks
and put in a saucepan. Grate off a teaspoon
of orange rind, then squeeze the orange
juice. Add the rind, juice and sugar to the
apples and cook gently for about 10 minutes. Leave to cool.

Lightly whip the cream. Heat the butter
and oil and fry the breadcrumbs for a few
minutes until golden, turning them over as
they cook. Leave to cool on greaseproof
paper.

Put layers of apple, crumbs and cream in a
serving dish, ending with a layer of cream.

Serve at once, or chill for not more than 2
hours.

Variation
Use canned apricots instead of apples.
Drain them well and cut into small pieces.
Put the apricots in the bottom of the serving
dish, then add all the cream and finish with a
layer of crumbs.

Custard Pie

Approximate preparation time: 20
minutes (plus standing time)
Serves 4

175 g/6 oz shortcake or digestive
biscuits
75 g/3 oz butter
300 ml/½ pint thick custard, still
slightly warm
1 tablespoon clear honey
1 (312-g/11-oz) can mandarin
oranges or fresh tangerines

Put the biscuits in a polythene bag and
crush with a rolling pin – but not so finely
that they are powdered. Melt the butter and
mix with the crushed biscuits. Press into a
20-cm/8-inch flan tin or a shallow pie dish.
Leave to set in a cool place – but not the
refrigerator where biscuits could become
soggy.

Fill the biscuit flan with the custard. Cover
with cling film and leave until cold. Remove
the film.

Spread the honey over the custard and
top with oranges.

About oranges

For desserts: *choose sweet oranges
like the Jaffa, Navel or Valencia
variety. The smaller oranges are
seasonal: look out for satsumas between October and February and the
delicious sweet tangerines from October to March. Experiment with the
more unusual crossbreeds like ugli
fruit, a cross between a tangerine and
a grapefruit and ortanique a cross
between an ordinary orange and a
tangerine.*

Rich Chocolate Custard

Approximate preparation time: 10
minutes
Cooking time: 50 minutes
Serves 3–4

100 g/4 oz plain chocolate
150 ml/¼ pint plus 2 tablespoons
milk
5 tablespoons double cream
65 g/2½ oz castor sugar
4 egg yolks

Break up the chocolate and put it in a basin
over a pan of gently simmering water. When
the chocolate has melted, pour in the milk
and heat until well mixed. If you have a
double saucepan you could use it instead of
the basin over a pan.

Put the cream in a bowl with the sugar
and egg yolks. Mix together. Pour in the
chocolate milk mixture, stirring all the time.
Pour into an ovenproof dish. Stand the dish
in a baking tin and pour in enough water to
come halfway up the sides of the dish. Cook
in a cool oven (150°C, 300°F, Gas Mark 2)
for 50 minutes or until set. Leave to cool.

Eat within 1 day and keep chilled.

Variations

For a more elaborate dessert, whip up some
double cream with sugar and rum to taste.
Pipe over the top of the cold custard just
before serving.

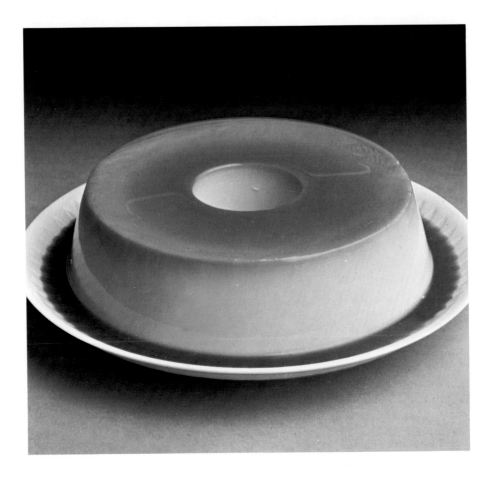

Caramel Custard

Approximate preparation time: 25
minutes (plus overnight standing)
Cooking time: 1 hour 6 minutes
Serves 4

150 g/5 oz castor sugar
600 ml/1 pint milk
2 large eggs, plus 2 large egg yolks
few drops vanilla essence

Put 75 g/3 oz of the sugar in a saucepan with 4 tablespoons cold water. Heat gently until the sugar dissolves then boil until golden brown. Pour into the base of a warmed ring mould.

Heat the milk without boiling. Mix the milk with the eggs, egg yolks, vanilla essence and remaining sugar. Pour into the mould and cover with foil.

Stand the mould in a roasting tin and pour in enough water to come halfway up the side of mould. Cook in a moderate oven (180°C, 350°F, Gas Mark 4) for 1 hour or until set. Leave in the mould overnight.

Turn out carefully on to serving plate and serve within 1 day.

Simple Savarin

Approximate preparation time: 30
minutes (plus standing time)
Cooking time: 20–25 minutes
Serves 4–5

100 g/4 oz plain flour
7 g/$\frac{1}{4}$ oz fresh yeast or
3 g/$\frac{1}{8}$ oz dried yeast
2 tablespoons lukewarm milk
40 g/1$\frac{1}{2}$ oz castor sugar
50 g/2 oz butter, softened
2 eggs
$\frac{1}{2}$ (425-g/15-oz) can peach halves
$\frac{1}{2}$ (227-g/8-oz) can pineapple chunks
$\frac{1}{2}$ (227-g/8-oz) can red cherries
100 g/4 oz blackberries
$\frac{1}{2}$ (298-g/10$\frac{1}{2}$-oz) can mandarin
oranges
2 tablespoons rum

Sift the flour into a large bowl. Cream the fresh yeast with the milk. If you are using dried yeast, follow the directions on the packet for activating – but still use 2 tablespoons of liquid.

Mix the yeast into the flour with the sugar, butter and eggs. Beat thoroughly to make a batter.

Grease an 18-cm/7-inch ring mould. Pour the batter into the mould and leave to stand in a warm place for 45 minutes to 1 hour or until the batter has risen to the top of the mould.

Cook the savarin in a hot oven (230°C, 450°F, Gas Mark 8) for 5 minutes, then turn down to moderately hot (200°C, 400°F, Gas Mark 6) and cook for a further 15–20 minutes or until firm. Turn out to cool on a wire rack.

This savarin does not have the traditional glaze which soaks into the cake. Simply mix all the fruit with 3 tablespoons of the peach juice and rum. Leave to stand for 2 hours. Don't use a metal dish.

Pile the soaked fruit into the savarin.

Eat within 1 day and keep in a cool place.

Strawberry Savarin

Approximate preparation time: 35
minutes (plus standing time)
Cooking time: 25–30 minutes
Serves 4

100 g/4 oz plain flour
7 g/$\frac{1}{4}$ oz fresh yeast or
3 g/$\frac{1}{8}$ oz dried yeast
2 tablespoons lukewarm milk
40 g/1$\frac{1}{2}$ oz castor sugar
50 g/2 oz butter, softened
2 eggs
50 g/2 oz granulated sugar
225 g/8 oz strawberries
300 ml/$\frac{1}{2}$ pint double cream,
whipped

Sift the flour into a large bowl. Cream the yeast with the milk. If using dried yeast, follow the directions on the packet, still using the 2 tablespoons of milk.

Add the yeast to the flour with the castor sugar, butter and eggs. Beat very thoroughly. Put the batter in a greased 18-cm/7-inch ring mould. Leave to stand in a warm place for 30–45 minutes or until the batter has risen to the top of the tin.

When the batter has risen, cook in a hot oven (230°C, 450°F, Gas Mark 8) for 5 minutes, then turn down to moderately hot (200°C, 400°F, Gas Mark 6) and cook for a further 15–20 minutes, or until firm to touch.

To prepare the syrup, put the granulated sugar in a small pan with $\frac{1}{2}$ cup of water. Heat gently until the sugar dissolves then boil for a few minutes until syrupy, but not changing colour.

Put the savarin on a wire rack with a plate underneath. Prick all over with a fork and pour the syrup on top. Leave to cool. Fill with the strawberries and cream.

Eat the same day.

Variations
Soak the strawberries for 1 hour in strawberry liqueur or apricot or cherry-flavoured brandy before filling the savarin.

Savarin au Rhum

Approximate preparation time: 30
minutes (plus standing time)
Cooking time: 43 minutes
Serves 6–8

25 g/1 oz fresh yeast or 1 teaspoon
dried yeast
6 tablespoons lukewarm milk
225 g/8 oz strong plain flour
$\frac{1}{2}$ teaspoon salt
2 tablespoons castor sugar
4 eggs
100 g/4 oz butter, softened
8 tablespoons clear honey
4 tablespoons rum
glacé cherries and angelica to
decorate
whipped cream to serve

Lightly grease a 2-litre/3$\frac{1}{2}$-pint ring mould. Put the yeast, milk and 50 g/2 oz of the flour in a bowl and beat until smooth. Allow to stand in a warm place until frothy, about 20 minutes.

Add the remaining flour, salt, sugar, eggs and butter to the mixture and beat well for 3–4 minutes. Turn into the tin and allow to rise until two-thirds full. Cook in a moderately hot oven (200°C, 400°F, Gas Mark 6) for about 40 minutes, until golden and shrinking away from the sides of the tin.

Turn out and leave to cool on a wire rack. Warm the honey with 150 ml/$\frac{1}{4}$ pint water and add the rum. Spoon over the savarin and soak well. Decorate with the cherries and angelica and serve with cream.

Variations
Instead of decorating the ring with glacé fruits, you can fill the centre with fresh fruit and cream. When strawberries are in season, pile them up, with cream between the layers, in the middle of the ring.

The cream can be coloured pink with a few drops of edible food colouring. In the winter months, a purée of cooked dried apricots could be used. Soak the apricots overnight in cold water then cook in the soaking water until tender. Drain and sieve to make a purée, sweeten to taste and use with cream to fill the centre of the ring.

Coconut Delight

Approximate preparation time: 25
minutes
Cooking time: 40–50 minutes
Serves 4

100 g/4 oz soft margarine
100 g/4 oz castor sugar
2 large eggs
100 g/4 oz self-raising flour
1 (425-g/15-oz) can peach slices
300 ml/½ pint double cream,
whipped
50 g/2 oz desiccated coconut
shredded coconut, toasted, for
decoration

For speed, this cake is made in an electric mixer. Line a deep, round 20-cm/8-inch cake tin with greaseproof paper. Lightly grease the paper.

Cream the margarine and sugar in the mixer until very pale and fluffy, then beat in the eggs. Fold in the flour using a metal spoon. Turn the mixture into the prepared tin. Smooth the top with a palette knife and cook in a moderate oven (180°C, 350°F, Gas Mark 4) for 40–50 minutes, or until cooked – it should feel firm to the touch and shrink away from edge of tin. Turn out and cool on a wire rack.

Split the cake in two. Keep a few peach slices for decoration and use the rest with most of the cream and desiccated coconut to sandwich the cake together again. Top with the remaining cream, peach slices and shredded coconut.

Serve within 4 hours of adding the cream and keep in a cold place.

Fruit Casket

Approximate preparation time: 25
minutes
Cooking time: 40–45 minutes
Serves 4–6

100 g/4 oz butter
100 g/4 oz castor sugar
2 teaspoons grated orange rind
2 large eggs
100 g/4 oz self-raising flour
150 g/5 oz strawberries
150 g/5 oz raspberries
25 g/1 oz brown sugar
300 ml/½ pint double cream
rum to taste

Grease a deep 19-cm/7½-inch cake tin. Line with greaseproof paper.

Put the butter and the castor sugar in a mixing bowl. Add the orange rind and beat until light and fluffy. Beat the eggs then gradually beat into the creamed mixture. Fold in the flour using a metal spoon. Turn the mixture into the prepared tin. Smooth the top with a palette knife. Cook the cake in a moderate oven (180°C, 350°F, Gas Mark 4) for 40–45 minutes or until firm to the touch and beginning to shrink away from the sides of the tin. Turn out to cool on a wire rack.

Split the sponge, near the top, almost in two, leaving one side intact like a hinge. Fill with the strawberries and raspberries and sprinkle with the sugar. Whip the cream and flavour with the rum. Pipe the cream on to the top.

Eat the same day.

Raspberry Flan

Approximate preparation time: 30 minutes
Cooking time: 10–15 minutes
Serves 4

1 large egg
50 g/2 oz castor sugar
50 g/2 oz self-raising flour
175 g/6 oz raspberries
4 tablespoons double cream,
whipped

Lightly grease a 21-cm/$8\frac{1}{2}$-inch sponge flan tin.

Use an electric whisk to mix the egg with the sugar, continuing until the mixture is thick and fluffy. Sift the flour over the top and fold in with a metal spoon.

Turn the mixture into the prepared tin and cook in a moderately hot oven (190°C, 375°F, Gas Mark 5) for 10–15 minutes, or until well risen and golden. Turn out and cool on a wire rack.

Fill the cooled flan with the raspberries and pipe a whirl of cream in the centre of the flan. Eat the same day.

Non-stick tins
If you are using non-stick cake tins, check the mixture towards the end of the cooking time to see that it does not overcook. These tins, although excellent and labour-saving, do tend to be rather thin, so the mixture may cook more quickly than in an ordinary tin.

If you invest in non-stick bakeware, you won't need to grease or line the tins, but you will need to treat them carefully and follow the manufacturer's instructions for washing and looking after them.

No-bake Party Cake

Approximate preparation time:
25 minutes (plus standing time)
Serves 4–6

175 g/6 oz digestive biscuits
75 g/3 oz unsalted butter
25 g/1 oz castor sugar
1 medium banana
juice of 1 small orange
150 ml/$\frac{1}{4}$ pint double cream
1 tablespoon whisky
225 g/8 oz green grapes
350 g/12 oz strawberries

Reduce the biscuits to coarse crumbs in a liquidiser or by beating with a rolling pin. Melt the butter and mix with the crumbs and sugar. Use this mixture to line the base and sides of a 20-cm/8-inch flan dish. Leave to set in a cool place.

Slice the banana and toss quickly in the orange juice to prevent discoloration.

Whip the cream with the whisky and spread it over the base of the flan. Arrange the fruit on top in a pattern. Serve within 4 hours of assembling, and keep cool, but not in the refrigerator.

Variations
For an extra-rich dessert, melt 50 g/2 oz plain chocolate and spoon it over the cooled biscuit base. Allow to set before adding the cream. If liked, replace the whisky with a coffee-flavoured liqueur or a peach or apricot brandy.

No-bake Party Cake

Gingernut Pie

Approximate preparation time: 20
minutes (plus standing time)
Serves 3–4

175 g/6 oz gingernut biscuits
75 g/3 oz butter
150 ml/¼ pint evaporated milk,
chilled
2 teaspoons finely grated lemon
rind
tiny gingernuts for decoration
crystallised ginger
100 g/4 oz black grapes, halved and
pips removed

Put the biscuits in a polythene bag and crush with a rolling pin – they should be fine crumbs, but not powdery.

Melt the butter and mix with the crushed biscuits. Press into a 20-cm/8-inch flan tin or shallow dish. Leave to set, but not in refrigerator where it might become soggy. Whisk the chilled milk until thick, stir in lemon rind and spoon into the flan.

Decorate with tiny gingernuts, if you have them, or small pieces of crystallised ginger and grapes.

Serve the same day.

Variations
For a less rich flan, replace the gingernuts with digestive biscuits. A really refreshing topping fo this pie would be slices of red-skinned apple, cored but not peeled and tossed in a little lemon juice to prevent discoloration. Cut the lemon rind into very fine shreds and use as a decoration – just scatter over the top of the apples before serving.

Chocolate Crispie

Approximate preparation time: 10
minutes (plus standing time)
Serves 2–3

1½ cups cornflakes
75 g/3 oz plain chocolate
1 large banana
2 tablespoons lemon juice
225 g/8 oz strawberries

Put the cornflakes in a small, shallow serving dish. Break up the chocolate into small pieces and put in the top of a double saucepan. When the chocolate has melted, mix it with the cornflakes and leave in a cold place (but not the refrigerator) for 2 hours.

Peel and slice the banana. Toss the slices in the lemon juice and mix with the strawberries (halved if they are very large) and pile on top of the cornflakes.

Serve at once.

Variations
Fill the chocolate case with a layer of canned cream and cover with slices of fresh orange brushed with honey.

INDEX

154

155